Welcome to the world of diving! I hope this sport brings you as many good times and memories as it has me!

This book is written for divers of all levels of certification and skill. Whether you're about to take your first class —or are a seasoned "bug" hunter—this book should have some information for you.

Each chapter can stand alone and be read out of sequence if you desire. So...happy reading, happy dives... and I'll see you underwater!

Paul McCallum

ACKNOWLEDGMENTS

Without these people in my life, this book might not have been written.

"Flipper," for inspiration.

Charlie, who bought me my first set of dive gear eighteen years ago.

Nikki Vaughan, who introduced me to underwater photography.

Cory Greenfield, my first dive buddy.

Jon Hardy, friend and dive companion, the man who trained me to be an instructor.

Rocky, Jill, Shawn, and Pete at bank of Scubahaus, for keeping me and my gear working.

Barry Krause, for suggesting I write this book.

Howard Hall, who took me on my first shark dives, and whose book has been a source of inspiration.

Lorraine Sadler, friend, model, and companion on many memorable dives.

NAUI, for allowing me to reproduce their dive tables for illustration purposes.

Charles "Chipper" Pastron, the most enthusiastic diver on the planet, and sole creator of the Osborn Bank fashion line.

Jay O'Donnell, the driest diver I know.

David McCallum, my "computer doctor."

Steve Joyner and Marva Hurst, for their assistance in the preparation of this manuscript.

My family.

Christine Lariviere McCallum, for putting up with hotels filled with wet dive gear—bathrooms filled with wet camera gear—and a house filled with divers, photographers, treasure hunters, writers, pilots, and magazine editors! I love you!

THE
Scuba Diving
HANDBOOK

A Complete Guide
to Salt and Fresh Water Diving

Paul M\^cCallum

BETTERWAY PUBLICATIONS, INC.
WHITE HALL, VIRGINIA

Published by Betterway Publications, Inc.
P.O. Box 219
Crozet, VA 22932
(804) 823-5661

Cover design by Rick Britton
Photographs by Paul McCallum and Howard Hall
Cover photo: Sponges and other marine growths grow on the
bow gun of the *Fijikawa Maru* in Truk Lagoon.
Typography by Typecasting

It is impossible to learn to scuba dive solely from a book. Competent
instruction from a certified instructor is also necessary. Any depth
and time limits set in this text should only be used as guidelines.
Neither the author nor Betterway Publications, Inc. accepts any
responsibility for how this information is interpreted or used.

Library of Congress Cataloging-in-Publication Data

McCallum, Paul
    The scuba diving handbook : a complete guide to salt and fresh
water diving / Paul McCallum.
        p.   cm.
    Includes bibliographical references and index.
    ISBN 1-55870-180-X: $19.95
    1. Scuba diving—Handbooks, manuals, etc. I. Title.
GV840.S78M3927 1991
797.2′3—dc20
                                                    90-21714
                                                       CIP

Printed in Canada
0 9 8 7 6 5 4 3 2 1

This Book is dedicated to
Jill Ireland Bronson
and
Jason David McCallum

Contents

1. Why Dive? 9
2. Getting Certified 19
3. Dive Stores 25
4. Equipment 29
5. Theory 43
6. Dive Tables 53
7. Self-Sufficient Diver 71
8. Emergency Procedures And First Aid 81
9. Dive Specialties 95
10. Cooking What You Catch 110
11. Photography 121
12. Dive Travel 135
13. Marine Life 155
14. Fresh Water 163
15. Dive Computers 169
16. Periodicals 179
Glossary 183
Index 187

CHAPTER 1

Why Dive?

Why dive? Here are ten reasons why I think *you* should become a scuba diver!

Adventure

Imagine exploring a submerged World War II wreck in the South Pacific. Or how about swimming eye to eye with a whale. Or have you ever fantasized about what it would be like to go underwater in a shark cage and see sharks up close?

The first time I saw a really large animal underwater I wasn't expecting it. Some friends and I had gone diving to try to photograph the octopi we had consistently seen off Westard Beach just north of Malibu, California. Towards the end of the dive while I was trying to lure a shy octopus out from its den, my buddy Jay O'Donnell began tugging enthusiastically on my leg. My first reaction was to ignore him since the octopus I'd been working with was beginning to co-operate...and I was sure he simply wanted to point out another photo opportunity. Jay, determined to get my attention, kept tugging so I swam out from under the ledge to see what all the excitement was about; the look on his face made me worry. Wide-eyed and shocked he was looking directly behind me with fear in his eyes. When I spun around to see what he was looking at, I thought, "My God, that's the biggest shark on the planet!"

The shadow moving directly toward us was over 30 feet long and traveling faster than anything I had ever seen in the ocean. After a few tense moments I realized we were about to be eye to eye with a California Grey Whale—not a record-size great white shark!

The whale kept moving toward us until it passed not more than 10 feet in front of me. Charles Bisharat, our third dive buddy that day, had already surfaced and was watching the scene unfold from above. He later described how amazing it was to see the two divers become dwarfed as the whale swam by.

Looking back on that moment the two things that stand out in my mind are the silence of it and the whale's eye. As the whale swam by it looked at me...and it was the same type of look you get from a person; you could see intelligent thought taking place. Just the opposite of a shark's eye, which is cold and unreadable.

The fact that the whale was moving through the water in total silence gave the encounter a feeling of timelessness—it felt as if time stood still for a few moments.

As the whale moved off, I became aware of a voice in my head screaming, "CAMERA!" Unfortunately, I was too overcome with awe to react quickly enough, and so missed capturing the whale on film.

One of my most adventure-filled dives was the first time I went shark-diving. I would like to point out that I never saw a shark during my first thirteen years as diver. It wasn't until I actually went out and put bait in the water to draw the sharks in that I saw one.

Standing on the boat's swim step, 10 miles off the coast of San Diego with over 2000 feet of water below me—while preparing to jump into an ocean where over forty blue sharks were swimming around looking for the source of the blood they could smell in the water—was definitely a high adrenaline experience!

Once in the water I don't think my senses have ever been as heightened as they were during the 80-foot swim through the open water to the shark cage.

Anyone with basic scuba diving skills can partake in adventures such as these.

Relaxation

Moments in my life when I have felt the most at peace have been directly associated with my dive experiences. A calm day spent snorkeling in the shallow lagoons off the Islands of Palau, sitting on a boat in Truk lagoon watching incredible sunsets, or at the end of a day of diving, having dinner on the beach on Grand Cayman Island are all memorable moments because of the feeling of tranquility that was present.

On a recent dive off Catalina Island, I spent forty-five minutes lying on the bottom of the ocean, watching a large California bat ray that had settled in front of me. At first the animal was apprehensive about my presence, but after five minutes or so, it allowed me to approach within 5 feet. Few things are as relaxing as moments like this; job pressures, personal problems, and financial worries are all forgotten as you become immersed in the marine environment.

Exercise

Swimming is recognized as an excellent form of exercise. Your cardiovascular system gets a workout and muscles become toned.

But swimming endless repetitive laps in a pool quickly becomes mundane. Many people start a swimming program filled with good intentions and long-range fitness goals, only to quit after a few weeks because of boredom.

When I go diving, exercise is not my primary motive, but I do like the fact that I get exercise while doing something I enjoy! I find most gyms overcrowded, boring, and confining and I don't like using equipment that someone else has just dripped sweat all over. Wouldn't you rather spend an enjoyable day in the sun and surf?

Travel

My interest in diving has led to my discovery of tropical paradises most people have never visited. Truk Lagoon in the South Pacific is home to a ghost fleet of sixty-six Japanese ships that were sunk in a three-day period during World War II. Many people are unaware of Truk's existence.

I recently went to Hawaii with a group of non-divers. We spent a few days hiking up to volcanoes and exploring the island's interior. Being a diver enabled me to go and explore the underwater world of the islands. Being a scuba diver in

An American Hellcat lies abandoned in the South Pacific.

a foreign land opens doors unavailable to your non-diving companions.

With a little ingenuity you may discover free travel benefits by selling your diving skills. Many of my friends are part-time underwater photographers. One of these guys constantly amazes us with the complimentary hotel rooms, discounted air fares, and free boat rides he obtains in exchange for a few underwater photos. Any water-related resort business that publishes a brochure or some kind of promotional material is usually receptive to what underwater photographers have to offer.

See Wild Animals

No matter where you live there is probably an ocean, lake, or pond nearby. With minimal financial investment you can observe unusual underwater wildlife in its native habitat. Scuba diving opens this door for you.

If you want to go see lions and tigers in the wild, you are going to have to spend a lot of money and travel to some hard-to-reach destination. The whale described previously was seen 200 feet off the coast of southern California! A business

Learning to scuba dive opens the door to underwater adventures such as this close-up encounter with an angel shark in 130 feet of water.

man who works in downtown Los Angeles could literally go diving with wild California whales at the end of his work day! He could not visit wild elephants in their native habitat after a day's work.

No matter where you live, there's probably salt or fresh water wildlife waiting for your discovery a few miles from where you sit at this moment—go see them!

Because You Can

When my grandparents were my age, they couldn't have gone scuba diving even if they wanted to; the technology simply wasn't there. This is the first time in history that anybody with basic swimming skills can visit the underwater world. Going underwater a hundred years ago required the use of surface-supplied air that was delivered to the diver by way of a hose through which the air was pumped. A dangerous proposition at best! Modern scuba gear is safe, easy to use, reliable, comfortable, and affordable.

A hundred years from now, if the current pollution rate isn't altered, many of the animals that I see and take for granted during my dives will have become extinct. In the few short years that I have been diving, the pollution level in Santa Monica bay has risen to the extent that I no longer dive there because it is now considered unhealthful in some areas. Other areas of the world are experiencing similar rises in pollution. The St. Lawrence River in Montreal was clear and frequented by swimmers fifty years ago. Today, visibility in the river averages less than 2 feet, and health hazard signs are posted.

We are (in a sense) a lucky generation. This may be the only time in the history of our planet where the technology to explore underwater exists in combination with low-enough pollution levels to make the experience safe and enjoyable. In 200 years the thought of entering what may be horribly murky and polluted waters may be downright repulsive! Take advantage of the fact that you are alive during this golden moment in time and go diving!

Obviously, pollution can be reversed. But as history is usually an excellent teacher, I am not feeling very optimistic.

Make Money

I get about two calls a month from various places around the world that are looking for dive instructors. Most instructors I know are already too involved with projects to fill these positions.

Many of the dive industry publications have extensive "help wanted" advertisements. Dive masters are needed to supervise boats. Resorts often have turnover in personnel and most dive shops have three or four instructors on staff. Instruction aside, boat cleaning, light salvage work, and water safety duties are all opportunities that can be filled by a certified diver.

Occasionally, I do jobs supervising underwater sequences in feature films. Usually, there are insurance requirements as to how many "qualified" rescue divers must be present when a film company has people in the water. Inevitably much time on these jobs is spent lounging around on a boat, sipping Perrier. All in all, not a bad way to spend a few days!

Other duties a diver might have on a film might be as simple as standing by in the water while a stunt is executed. In the film *Assassination,* there was a stunt where a jet skier jumped over a speed boat, smashing the boat's windshield. To do this a ramp was built on the side of the boat opposite the camera (thus out of sight of the camera). One of my jobs was to ensure that the ramp wasn't pushed out of position by water movement. I had the best view of anyone as the jet skier flew directly overhead!

Most jobs like this have come to me simply because somebody on the film knew this guy (me) who was a diver!

Meet People

I met my wife four years ago while teaching a dive class. She wasn't in the class, but had come down to the beach with a friend to watch. Obviously, I think scuba diving is a great way to meet people!

While I can't guarantee that you'll meet a future husband or wife, it is safe to say that you'll meet a wide variety of people from every walk of life. Diving is a social activity; from your first scuba class on, you'll probably always be with at least a small group of people when you dive.

Dive boats range in size from small "six-packs" that take up to six people out for a day of diving, to the large boats that may have as many as forty-five people on board. You can't help getting to know people on boat dives since you're living in such small quarters.

Non-divers have a natural curiosity when they find out about your underwater activities. From your first dive on, you'll have stories to tell. If you were at a party and you had the choice of talking to a farmer, a lawyer, or the guy who discovered the *Titanic*, whom would you want to talk to? Telling people you're into diving is a terrific ice breaker.

Access to New Experiences

Learning how to dive is only the beginning. It's like getting a driver's license; once you have it you can get in the car and really go places. Once you become a certified diver, you'll have access to an endless list of new activities.

Three months ago while on assignment in Vanuatu in the South Pacific, I was diving and photographing the wreck

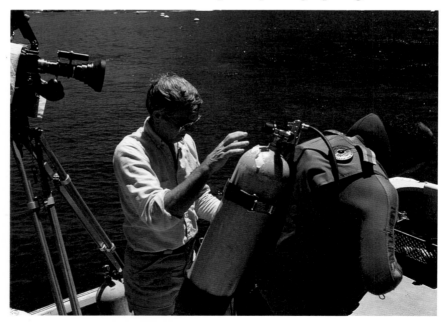

Jon Hardy assists cinematographer Marty Snyderman prepare for a dive during the filming of a documentary off Catalina Island. Film work, underwater photography, instruction, boat cleaning, and salvage work are only a few of the career opportunities that can be pursued by divers!

Diving can be enjoyed equally by both men and women.

Photographing inside a shipwreck requires extreme caution. This World War II vintage jeep was found inside one of the cargo holds of the President Coolidge.

of the *President Coolidge,* which sank in 1942. The *President Coolidge* is a 654-foot luxury liner that was converted into a troop carrier when the United States entered into World War II.

Swimming along one of the ship's corridors I noticed an unusual looking object lying on the bottom. After gently fanning the silt away, the shape of a hand gun became recognizable. Moments latter I was holding a pistol that had been used in World War II and had gone down with the ship almost fifty years ago!

A few months earlier, while diving off the islands of Palau, I found myself completely surrounded by a school of barracuda. Contrary to popular belief, these animals are not aggressive and aren't a threat to divers. The barracuda and I spent twenty minutes swimming circles around one another. I took their picture, they kept an eye on me, and my dive buddy took pictures of me photographing the barracuda.

Three days ago I was diving San Nicolas Island, 66 miles off the coast of southern California. When the boat prepared to drop anchor, we were immediately joined by a pod of about sixty sea lions. Since the animals seemed to be in a cooperative mood, I abandoned my original dive plan and grabbed a camera and entered the water without a tank (skin diving). The rest of the day was spent playing with the sea lions, swimming with sea lions, skin diving with sea lions, playing tag with sea lions, feeding sea lions. All in all, a very enjoyable day!

Once you've learned to dive, the list of new experiences you can have is endless.

Because It's Fun

This is the best reason of all!

CHAPTER 2

Getting Certified

To prevent people from hurting themselves, the scuba industry has a self-regulating *certification program*. If people didn't understand the dangers in using compressed air while underwater, they could hurt themselves. Without a certification card, dive stores will not sell you a scuba tank, regulator, or buoyancy control jacket, nor will they fill a tank unless the owner first presents a certification card.

To become a certified diver, you need to enroll in a course sanctioned by one of the certifying agencies. Three of the bigger agencies are NAUI, PADI, and SSI. There are also quite a few midsize agencies that offer competent instruction.

I recommend that you go with one of the above agencies because your card will be accepted by most stores and resorts in the world. If you have a card from "Barry's Diving School," chances are that dive masters are not going to accept your certification card as evidence that you have received competent instruction.

NAUI offers a full range of certification courses from Open Water I all the way up to Instructor. NAUI certification cards are basically accepted worldwide. NAUI's address is:

The National Association of Underwater Instructors
P.O. Box 14650
Montclair, CA 91763-1150
Phone: (714) 621-5801

A diver silhouetted by the tropical sun of the South Pacific.

PADI courses are also taught worldwide and the certification cards received in these courses are accepted practically everywhere. PADI's address is:

The Professional Association of Diving Instructors
1251 East Dire Road #100
Santa Ana, CA 92705-5605
Phone: (714) 540-7234

SSI is the smallest of these agencies, but follows basically the same standards as NAUI and PADI. Their certification cards are recognized around the world. SSI's address is:

Scuba Schools International
2619 Canton Court
Fort Collins, CO 80525
Phone: (303) 482-0883

You can write any one of the above agencies to receive a list of stores that teach the courses they sanction.

STANDARDS

All of these agencies have agreed on a set of *standards.* By following the same standards there is some form of unification as to what type of training students are receiving.

A newly-certified diver examines two large sea stars.

Sometimes an individual agency's standards are higher (in certain areas) than the other agencies. The standards ensure that a diver who takes a NAUI course is basically receiving the same type of information as a student who takes a PADI course. If you were to receive instruction from one of the smaller, unknown agencies, you might not receive instruction that is up to the minimum requirements followed by the rest of the industry.

As far as which agency you should go with, it is a personal choice; each one naturally thinks it is the best! Usually what it will come down to is what the store or resort offers. Whichever one you end up with, you can be assured that you will receive excellent instruction.

✦ PREREQUISITES FOR TRAINING

Anyone with competent swimming skills can become a certified scuba diver! To determine if your swimming skills are "competent," ask yourself the following question: If you were standing on the edge of a boat that was anchored in deep, calm, flat water, and you accidentally fell off—would you be in trouble? If the answer is yes, you might want to take a few swimming lessons before you enroll in a dive course!

Most certifying agencies require students to be a minimum of twelve years old before they can become trained as divers (one reason is the weight of the gear). Divers between the ages of twelve and fifteen receive a junior certification card (standards vary slightly between agencies). A junior certification is similar to a learner's permit when learning to drive; you may dive only when a certified adult diver is present.

BASIC COURSE CONTENTS

Scuba diving courses are broken up into three sections: Classroom, Pool, and Open Water.

CLASSROOM. Lectures, slide and video presentations, and tests will all be presented in the classroom portion of your course. "Classroom" is a very loose term when it comes to diving courses; your classroom may be a beach or by the side of a pool in some instances.

POOL. It is safer for you to be introduced to new diving skills in the confined, controlled environment of a swimming pool.

Your first pool session will probably include a swimming test. The swimming test generally consists of: 1. A distance swim, 2. Swimming underwater (breath hold), and 3. Treading water for some predetermined amount of time. Other skills will include getting water out of your mask, taking equipment on and off, emergency procedures, and a variety of other skills.

It is possible to teach a dive course exclusively in the ocean and not use a pool at all. A nearby lagoon may be shallow and calm enough that it is used in lieu of a pool.

OPEN WATER. When you get to the open water segment of your training, you will be diving in local conditions! If you live inland, you may be diving in a lake; if you live in a coastal city, you will be diving in the open water of an ocean.

Open water is where it all comes together, and the more time spent actually diving in the conditions you will encounter after certification, the better! Keep that in mind when comparing courses taught at different stores; you want the one that offers the most open water dives.

HOW LONG DOES IT TAKE?

To complete a basic certification course will take between twenty-four and forty-eight hours of your time; this will be divided between the pool, classroom, and open water sessions. It is possible to do it in less time, but you can use this as a base for the amount of time you will spend.

A common itinerary is to space the course out over four weeks. You may meet on Tuesday and Thursday nights for classroom and pool sessions and go to the beach on either Saturday or Sunday mornings. This routine would be repeated four times. Private instruction on the other hand allows you to set up your classes around your own schedule.

✦ THE RESORT COURSE

Most dive resorts offer some type of resort course/scuba experience. This is *not* a certification course, but is designed to give somebody with no previous experience "a taste" of what diving is like.

A resort course may not have any classroom or pool sessions. Participants are given minimum instruction and are then taken diving. Obviously, these courses are done in shallow, calm conditions similar to those of a pool.

Dive instructors should be friendly and should make your scuba experience enjoyable!

CHAPTER 3

Dive Stores

Like divers themselves, dive stores come in all shapes and sizes and provide a variety of services. A small store aboard a ship may primarily rent equipment and not provide instruction or have spare parts. A large retail outlet may—in addition to selling and renting gear—provide instruction, have an in-store dive club, and even own its own dive boat. Since your relationship with the store usually continues once you become certified, it is important to pick a store that will be able to meet all of your needs.

If you live in an area where diving is not a popular sport and/or there is not a diveable body of water nearby, you may not have a choice as to which store you go to. If there is only one dive store within a hundred miles of where you live, then it would be impractical to go elsewhere. If you are, however, fortunate enough to have a selection of stores to choose from, here are some things you should consider.

⬥ LOCATION

Besides the obvious consideration of where the store is located in relation to where you live, you should also consider where they conduct their classes. During your certification course, you will spend a few nights listening to lectures about various aspects of diving. Some stores conduct the lecture part of their courses on the premises while others may rent classrooms several miles away.

You should ask the same location questions about the pool that will be used during your dive training. I know of one store where the classroom, the pool, and the place students must pick up their gear (usually at the store) are all 30 miles away from each other! A lot of driving, especially if you were not aware of it when you signed up, can be irritating.

RENTAL DEPARTMENT

Is the equipment in the store's rental department modern and safe? Naturally, if you have not yet received any training, you will not be able answer this question yourself, so when you go visit the shop, it might be a good idea to have a certified friend come along to have a look. If you don't have a certified friend, try asking the store how often they replace and/or overhaul their rental gear. Scubahaus (in Santa Monica, California), for example, completely overhauls all gear at six month intervals, while another store (which will remain nameless) only services their gear "when it breaks"!

The other consideration is do they *guarantee* that students in their classes will have equipment available to them? I once taught at a store that would over-book the number of students scheduled for training dives, with the result that students would come to pick up their gear and there wouldn't be any left, though it had been previously reserved. With most established stores, this is not a problem, but it can happen.

You should also check that they have your size in stock. While you may be guaranteed that equipment will be available, if you are unusually short or tall they may not have a wetsuit, for example, that will fit you.

STUDENT INCENTIVES

A lot of dive stores offer some type of discount for students who enroll in their classes once they have become certified. Scubahaus, for example, offers 10% off all equipment bought by students who have taken one of their courses.

While this shouldn't necessarily be expected, it could be a deciding factor if you are trying to decide between two or three stores.

DO THE INSTRUCTORS WORK AT THE STORES?

I think you should take classes from instructors who work

for a dive store. (Naturally, there are exceptions to this rule and I acknowledge that there are a lot of excellent independent instructors out there.) The reason is that an instructor who works at the store knows what rental equipment is available, what the store sells, and generally is more involved in diving than someone who only teaches diving part-time. Who would you rather trust your life to—a full time scuba instructor or a car salesman (for example) who teaches diving in "his spare time"?

✦ TYPE OF STORE

Does the store specialize exclusively in scuba diving, or does it sell a wide variety of water sport equipment? For some stores, scuba diving may be only a small portion of their overall business. Water skiing, wind surfing, jet skiing, canoeing, kayaking, and a host of other water activities may constitute the rest of their operation.

It is better to deal with a store that specializes in diving exclusively.

✦ SERVICE

Does the store have a reputation for servicing equipment once purchased? Dive gear requires periodic maintenance. If the store doesn't have qualified, in-house repair people, they will have to send the equipment back to the manufacturer, which can be costly and time-consuming.

All dive stores should have compressors on the premises (to fill the tanks). While this is usually a standard piece of equipment, I have encountered a few stores that had no means of filling dive tanks. All of these stores, by the way, were of the multi-sport type.

Does the store carry a wide selection of gear and does it carry name brand products? A little asking around or thumbing through dive magazines will give you an idea of what some of the established brand names in the industry are.

✦ PERSONNEL / PERSONALITY

Do you feel comfortable with the salespeople and instructors associated with the store? Scuba diving is a recreational sport and should be fun!

Diver training originated in the military and evolved into recreational courses designed for civilians. Unfortunately, some militaristic intimidation training procedures still exist with some instructors. If you encounter an instructor who makes you feel intimidated, I suggest you move on to someone else.

You are going to spend a considerable amount of money when you purchase a complete set of dive gear. Store personnel should be courteous and spend a reasonable amount of time answering your questions and explaining the various features on different types of gear.

DON'T SHOP BY MAIL

If you are not already a certified diver, I recommend that you don't shop by mail. Your life may depend on the quality of the gear you use. While advertised discount prices in some of the magazines may seem attractive, in the long run it is better to buy at a store where you can be assured of service should something go wrong. Also, if you are not yet certified, you don't know what the pros and cons are of certain types of gear.

A housed camera system allows you to take close-up shots like this group of strawberry anemones.

CHAPTER 4

Equipment

The number of active divers in the United States has grown enormously in the last five years. A few years ago my dive classes had an average of one woman to every seven men. I now teach as many women as men, and one of the reasons for these changes is the recent evolution of gear design.

Dive gear has made tremendous progress in the last decade in the areas of comfort, fit, and ease of use. A few years ago, diving was limited to a few hardy souls willing to endure painful and cumbersome gear. Color has also become a selling point. Whereas everything used to be black, now if you want a pink and lime green wetsuit, you can have it.

Dive shops generally refer to masks, fins, and snorkels as personal gear. This is because most shops don't rent these items but expect you to buy them when enrolling in a diving class. Expect to spend between $150 and $250 for your personal gear (also referred to as "skin diving gear"). A reputable dealer will let you return anything that doesn't fit. Items can usually be tried in a pool and returned, but once you take something into the ocean, you own it due to the fact that the gear is more prone to scuff marks from rocks and boat decks.

MASKS

The main reason you want to go scuba diving (or snorkeling) is to see what's under the water's surface. This makes mask selection very important. All of the other gear that you purchase will be used to sustain your body underwater while you look around. Considering this, take your time when selecting your mask.

To tell if a mask fits, do the following: Hold the mask up to your face and inhale. Don't use the mask strap when you do this. If the mask sticks to your face, it fits. If it doesn't, air is leaking in and preventing a seal. Where the air is coming in is where water will enter the mask while you are diving.

Any dive mask you buy should be made of shatterproof glass. If it doesn't say so on the face plate, ask a salesperson and make sure it is. This is to prevent the mask from imploding if you should accidentally crack the glass under water.

Masks are referred to as *high volume* or *low volume,* indicating the amount (volume) of air space inside the mask. Masks with side ports increase your field of vision, and are high volume. Low volume masks usually have a limited field of vision. The volume inside a mask is a consideration when learning how to clear the mask.

Clearing your mask means to remove the water out of it while underwater. This is done by blowing out of your nose while holding the bottom of your mask away from your face. As the air fills the mask, it pushes the water out of the bottom of the mask. A high volume mask can hold more water than a low volume mask, so it might take you two breaths to clear a high volume mask, but only one breath to clear a low volume mask. There's nothing wrong with taking two breaths to clear your mask; it's just that some people are uncomfortable with water on their face that long.

Some masks have a *purge valve.* This device allows you to clear water out of the mask by simply looking down and blowing out your nose. I recommend that you avoid purge valves for two reasons. One, they tend to leak after a while and need replacing, and two, if you rely on the purge valve to clear the mask, your mask clearing skills may become weak. Eventually, you may have to deal with your mask becoming fully flooded, but if you learned to clear your mask in the traditional manner this won't faze you.

Dive masks are designed so you can pinch your nose with your thumb and first finger of one hand. It is important that you can comfortably do this since this is how you will clear your ears. If you'll be wearing gloves, make sure the finger pockets are large enough to accommodate them. You need to be able to seal your nose well enough to prevent any air from coming out when you exhale.

Two other considerations are the type of buckles used and whether the mask is made of rubber or silicone. Old style metal buckles are hard to use, but are cheap to manufacture. Modern buckles can be adjusted without taking the mask off, and are spring-loaded, making them effortless to use. Basically, if you can afford it, get the better buckles. Same thing with rubber versus silicone: Rubber costs less than silicone, but rots quicker. Expect to pay between $30 and $100 for a good mask.

FINS

The type of fins you use must match the environment you dive in. If you dive in cold water, you'll be wearing a lot more gear than if you dive in warm water. The added gear creates drag, which requires a larger, stiffer fin.

There are three basic styles of fins currently on the market: the small body surfing fins ($10–30); full foot fins ($20–65); and fins with heel straps ($25–100).

As their name implies, the smaller fins are designed for use by body surfers and boogie boarders. Due to their small size and flexibility, they aren't capable of generating the propulsion required by divers. These types of fins are about half the size of fins designed for scuba and should be avoided.

Scuba diving fins come in two forms: full foot and heel strap. Full foot fins are worn like shoes. Your whole foot goes into the fin and there is no retaining device other than the resistance of the rubber. With heel strap fins, only the front two-thirds of your foot goes into the fin, and a heel strap holds your foot in place. Heel strap fins require *booties* to be worn to obtain a proper fit. The booties also insulate against the cold. Heel strap fins are used by cold water divers exclusively for this reason. Full foot fins (no bootie needed) are used by divers in tropical waters. Keep this in mind when buying your fins. If you're headed for the tropics, you may want to skip the added expense of booties.

Some fins have a *vent* on the blade. These are designed to allow water to pass through the vent when kicking in one direction, and to seal when kicking in the other. This translates into less strength needed to move the fin (the "cost" being less propulsion). If you haven't done a lot of swimming before, or have weak legs, you might want to consider this feature.

Heel strap fins will have some type of adjustable buckle. The spring-loaded types are easiest to use (but cost the most). Spend some time and make sure you can operate the buckle easily.

⌃ BOOTIES

The two features to be considered when buying booties are type of sole and whether or not you want a zipper. The better the sole, the more protection (and higher cost). Consider where you'll be diving. Beach divers may want added foot protection, while boat divers may not.

Zippers make the bootie a lot easier to put on at a cost of less warmth. Some dive boats in California don't allow you to wear your booties in the galley area. Situations like this, in which you are taking your booties off after every dive, are made more bearable with zippers. The beach is one location

This steel mesh shark suit is a specialized piece of equipment that allows divers to be bitten without fear of injury.

where zippers are a mistake. If you don't have a way to rinse sand off the zipper, the sand jams it, making it impossible to unzip.

Expect to pay between $20 and $70 for a pair of booties.

⬩ SNORKELS

Three features to consider when buying a snorkel are: 1. diameter; 2. whether you want a purge valve; and 3. adjustability.

Snorkels with a small diameter have a greater breathing resistance. It's like trying to suck air through a straw. Swimming on the surface while wearing full dive gear can be a workout, and using a small bore snorkel can make you feel

A student diver in full gear.

like you're not getting enough air, which may cause a feeling of anxiety and lead to other problems.

Purge valves will make the snorkel easier to clear, but also increase the price. They work because water seeks its own level. When you surface after a dive, the water in the snorkel above water level drains through the purge. When you clear the snorkel, you only have half as much water to blow out.

Another feature that affects snorkel price is how adjustable the mouth piece is. This doesn't affect the function of the snorkel, it just makes is more comfortable to use.

Expect to pay between $10 and $40 for a snorkel.

GLOVES

You may want to buy a pair of gloves ($10–65) when purchasing your personal gear. This is another piece of gear most shops don't rent.

If you're diving in cold water, it may be impossible to dive without them! Cold water gloves come with or without zippers. The same rules that applied to the zippers on booties apply to zippers on gloves.

Gloves also protect your hands from the environment. Rocks, sea urchins, fish spines, stinging corals, and shells are just a few of the possible hazards. If you're not diving in cold water, a pair of cheap work gloves may prove ideal.

The disadvantage to wearing gloves is a loss of sensitivity. It's harder to tell what you're touching if you can't see it. I don't like to wear gloves when I'm teaching. If I have to manipulate a student's buckle without being able to see it, I find the lost sense of feel annoying.

WETSUITS

A wetsuit doesn't prevent you from getting wet. What it does is hold a thin layer of water between your body and the suit. The layer of water gets warmed by your body heat and insulates you.

When trying wetsuits on, keep this in mind: anywhere there is a large air space inside the suit, cold water will circulate. This carries your body heat away and you will get chilled. With a wetsuit, comfort and fit are everything!

If you're diving in cold water, a good quality wetsuit should be your first major purchase once you become certified. Warm water divers have other priorities, but for cold water, start with a wetsuit.

A full cold water suit should consist of "Farmer John" style pants (looks like overalls) and a jacket. Cost for an off-the-rack suit will be in the $200 to $350 range. Some suits come with their own booties, hood, and gloves. The Farmer John style provides the most warmth due to the double layer of neoprene over the chest.

A *spine pad* is a strip of neoprene that is attached inside the Farmer John and runs down your spine. Its function is to fill up any space around the small of your back. Remember, anywhere there is an airspace, water will circulate and carry away body heat. A spine pad helps prevent this along your spine.

Knee pads are also desirable. If you're diving around rocks you'll notice the knees of your suit starting to show wear after a few dives. Knee pads slow down this process. I recommend not getting elbow pads because they make the arms of the suit stiffer.

Pockets are usually located on the upper thigh. Whether you want one or not is purely a personal decision. You can also get a pocket to hold your dive knife. Some divers don't like the added bulk that results from the addition of wetsuit pockets.

A step through jacket means that the suit top has short pant legs. This gives you double the insulation around your groin as well as your chest. If maximum warmth is your goal, this style suit may be for you.

Suits with plush lining are a lot easier to put on than suits lined with rubber and as you'd expect, this also makes the suit more expensive. You can also get a nylon outer layer, which makes the suit more durable (and more expensive).

If you want the best fit possible look into a custom-made suit. Prices start around $350 and go well over $1,000. One of the factors that can really drive the price up is fancy color schemes. I have two custom-made suits that are identical in cut and design, but radically different in color. One is all blue without any trim and cost me $465. My other suit is pink, with four different trim colors. It cost me $875. In case you are wondering, the blue suit is for working around sharks and the pink suit is so I can be quickly recognized as the instructor when teaching.

On boats dive gear may end up in one pile, so it's a good idea to mark your gear so it can be easily identified.

DRYSUITS

Drysuits, as their name implies, keep you dry. They have rubber seals around the neck and wrists, and the booties are a part of the suit. You wear some type of thermal underwear under the suit for additional warmth.

Drysuits cost more than wetsuits (prices start around $1,000) and require special training. Generally, they are not for beginners.

WEIGHT BELTS

Divers need to use weight to help overcome the buoyancy of their gear. The use of a full wetsuit, for example, makes it impossible to go underwater without the use of weights because the wetsuit adds volume without adding any substantial weight (see Archimedes' Principle, Chapter 5). This is why a diver may need twenty-five pounds of weight in California (where a thick full wetsuit is required because of the cold), but only six pounds when diving off Palau (no wetsuit required).

You buy the weights and the belt you put them on separately. There are two types of weights available. Uncoated lead is the cheapest (about $1.50 a pound). You can also get weights coated in plastic (about $2.50 a pound). Along with the standard designs the coated weights also come in unusual shapes such as hearts, hand grenades, and clam shells. When buying weights the thing to remember is that they are disposable! When you get in trouble, or are tired on a long swim, you may have to drop your weight belt. Don't spend so much money on your weight belt that you'll hesitate to ditch it if need be!

As you descend, your wetsuit compresses (see Boyle's Law, Chapter 5). Some weight belts are capable of compensating for this (about $30). If you're not wearing a full wetsuit (or if you don't want the added expense) you may want to go with a plain nylon web belt (about $10).

I also recommend you buy some weight belt keepers (about $1.50 each). These prevent the weights from sliding around on the belt. The idea is to keep the weights on your hip.

๙ TANKS

Scuba tanks are made of either steel or aluminum. Steel tanks are more prone to corrosion if salt water gets in them. Aluminum tanks have less of a problem with corrosion since steel tanks oxidize if salt water gets in them.

Both steel and aluminum tanks come in a variety of sizes. Aluminum tanks become positively buoyant when near empty (see Archimedes' Principle, Chapter 5). Both materials have advantages and disadvantages over each other. Which type you use depends on the type of diving you do. I use large volume tanks when I do deep dives, for example, but smaller tanks on beach dives where I want to cut down on the amount of weight I'm carrying.

All tanks have to be visually inspected once a year by a qualified inspector. If the tank passes, a sticker is put on the side of the tank showing the date of the inspection. Scuba tanks are hydrostatically tested every five years. If the tank passes, the date of the test is stamped on the side of the tank. If the "hydro" date is more than five years old, the tank is said to be "out of hydro." Tanks that are out of hydro are unsafe and cannot be filled until tested.

Tanks come in a variety of sizes. Don't make the mistake of getting a tank too large for you. Many women have been put off the sport by being given a tank that weighed too much for their body build. Tanks cost between $100 and $400.

ᴬ REGULATORS

A regulator is made up of two parts: the first stage, which is attached to the tank, and the second stage, which goes in your mouth.

The first stage has a series of ports for accessory hoses. At least one of these will be a high pressure port for the submersible pressure gauge that tells you how much air is in the tank.

The other ports are low pressure ports; they deliver air at a pressure of about 140 pounds per square inch (psi). It's important not to attach a low pressure accessory to a high pressure port since the high pressure port can be delivering air at a pressure as high as 3500 psi. If you do, you won't like the result.

Expect to pay between $150 and $500 for a regulator. One of the main features that affects price is whether or not the regulator is balanced. Simplified, a balanced regulator performs uniformly regardless of tank pressure, depth, or the attitude you're in (upside down, etc.). With an unbalanced regulator you'll notice an increase in breathing resistance under various situations. This isn't dangerous—it's just not as pleasant to use as a balanced regulator.

Some regulators have an adjustable second stage. This enables you to "fine tune" the amount of breathing resistance.

Regulator mouth pieces are available in different sizes. Be sure to get one that fits in your mouth comfortably.

ᴬ GAUGES

While diving, you will have to keep track of the following to be safe: how deep you are (Depth Gauge); how much air you have left (Submersible Pressure Gauge); how long you've been there (Bottom Timer); and where you are in relation to shore or your boat (Compass).

A depth gauge keeps track of your depth. If you're planning never to dive below 30 feet, one of the inexpensive (about $30) capillary gauges should be fine. These are based on Boyle's Law (see Chapter 5) and aren't very accurate below one atmosphere.

A good oil-filled depth gauge will run you about $100. A maximum depth indicator is a desirable feature. It's a second needle on the gauge that points to the deepest depth obtained during the dive. This is important to know when planning future dives in the day. Without this feature, you'll have to rely on memory after the dive.

Submersible pressure gauges (SPG's) will cost you between $50 and $150. It's important to get one that you can easily read since this is the gauge that tells you how much air you have left.

There are a variety of gauges to time the length of your dive (referred to as "bottom time"). A waterproof wristwatch is a bit of a bother since you have to remember what time you started your descent, what time you got out of the water, etc., but if you're on a budget and already own a watch, it will work.

A better solution is to use one of the combination bottom time/surface interval gauges available. These automatically keep track of how long your dive is, and how long you spend out of the water between dives. This information is important when working your dive tables (see Chapter 6). Cost is in the $100 range. I recommend the use of these timers since it eliminates the possibility of miscalculating (and becoming bent). Long swims on the surface with the added drag of dive gear can be tiring. A compass lets you keep track of where you are underwater, allowing you to return to your entry point underwater, avoiding long surface swims. Being lost underwater usually causes new divers a lot of anxiety; a compass (and learning how to use it) will help eliminate this.

I recommend you avoid the small watch band type compasses because they're too hard to see. A good underwater compass will cost you around $75. I highly recommend the Ikelite model; it's easy to read and fits in most consoles.

Most divers buy a gauge console that puts all your gauges at the end of your SPG hose. A fully equipped console will cost you between $200 and $400. There's a wide variety of consoles available, so take your time when looking. Some (like the Tekna) even have a dive knife on the back.

You can also pick the gauges you want and have console custom made to hold them. This allows you to put different brands in the same console. It also allows you to put all your gauges on one side of the console. Many of the commercial consoles put the compass on the back, which I find annoying because you have to turn the console over to see the compass.

The game bag hanging from this diver's belt can be used to carry a variety of items.

A custom console eliminates this. You can also put a slate and pencil on the back of your console to aid in communication.

COMPUTERS

Dive computers combine all the gauge functions into one unit. The advantage to computers is that along with supplying you with the needed information, they do the calculations for you, freeing you from worrying about dive tables. You simply look at your computer and it tells you how long you can stay down at any given depth. During the dive, the computer tells you how much time you have remaining. It will automatically adjust this time if your depth changes. Some computers (such as the Delphi by Orca) will calculate how much longer your air will last based on your current consumption rate. All in all, dive computers make diving safer. For more on computers see Chapter 15.

BUOYANCY COMPENSATORS

Buoyancy compensators—BC's in diver lingo—allow you to adjust your buoyancy while diving. Originally, they looked like the life vests currently used on airlines and were called

A dive knife is not used as a weapon, but as a tool. Chores such as cutting bait to feed fish are common.

"horse collar BC's." It's possible you could still encounter this style somewhere.

Modern BC's look like, and are worn like, jackets with the scuba tank strapped on the back. One of the nice features of these units is they can be easily slipped on and off. The BC can be filled with air from the scuba tank by using the power inflater, which is attached (by a hose) to the regulator's first stage.

You adjust your buoyancy by putting air in, or letting air out of, the BC. As you descend, you become more negatively buoyant because water pressure compresses your wetsuit, so you put air in your BC to establish neutral buoyancy. When you ascend toward the surface, you become more positively buoyant as the air in your BC expands due to reduced water pressure. A good BC will run you about $450.

Every time your depth changes, your buoyancy also changes; the idea is to be *neutrally* buoyant at any given depth.

KNIVES

The dive knife isn't worn for protection against predators of the deep, but is used for a variety of underwater chores. If you were to become entangled, for example, a sharp knife could be extremely useful!

A knife can also be used as a probe. If you want to see what is in a dark hole or nudge something out of the way, you may feel a lot safer doing it with a knife rather than your hand. A dive knife can cost anywhere from $20 to $100.

In case you are wondering, the idea of stabbing a shark is ridiculous. Even if you wanted to you wouldn't be able to do it; as you try to stab with the knife, you push yourself backwards rather than push the knife in.

UNDERWATER FLASH LIGHTS

Underwater lights can be divided into two categories. High Power Lights can be used for night diving, wreck diving, cave diving, or in any situation where maximum brightness is desired. Small Powered Lights are more portable and may be carried as backups or used during the day to peer into dark areas. Night diving in water with good visibility may require the use of a low-powered light. Dive lights cost between $50 and $100.

CHAPTER 5

Theory

Very few dive students retain the theory first taught during their entry level scuba course. When I first learned to dive, I retained very little of the theory. The problem with much of the theory is that it does not really apply in the real world of diving.

This chapter contains what you need to know to understand how pressure affects your body and equipment, and the why behind buoyancy. This is the core of what you need to know as far as practical knowledge. Understanding the forces that affect you while diving will make for safer, more comfortable, and more enjoyable diving.

⌁ PRESSURE

At sea level, the atmosphere exerts 14.7 pounds of pressure per square inch (psi). In other words, if you were to take a 1 inch square column of air that extended from sea level to the top of the measurable atmosphere (about 36,000 feet), it would weigh 14.7 pounds. This measurement, 14.7 psi, is referred to as 1 atmosphere (1 atm.) of pressure.

Because sea water is much denser (thus heaver) than air, it only takes 33 feet of sea water to exert a pressure of 1 atm (14.7 psi). So, 33 feet of sea water is said to exert 1 atm of pressure. Two times thirty-three is sixty-six, so 66 feet of sea water weighs 2 atm, and 99 feet weighs 3 atm and so on.

Ambient pressure refers to surrounding pressure, absolute pressure refers to the total of all pressure—such as water and atmosphere taken together. A diver at 99 feet is under 4 atm absolute pressure (3 water, and 1 surface).

↖ BOYLE'S LAW

Boyle's Law states that: as pressure increases, volume decreases ($P^+ = V^-$). It also applies in reverse. As pressure decreases, volume increases ($P^- = V^+$).

An example of Boyle's Law can be shown by taking a sponge in the palm of your hand and slowly closing your hand and squeezing the sponge. As your hand closes, pressure increases (P^+), and the volume of the sponge decreases (V^-). Slowly opening your hand will release the pressure (P^-), and the volume of the sponge increases (V^+).

Boyle's Law affects diving because of the pressure exerted by the water. The pressure volume change takes place in the air spaces contained in your body and equipment.

At 1 atm (33 feet), the pressure is great enough to compress air spaces to half their original volume. Let's say you had a one gallon plastic bottle, sealed it at the surface, and took it down to 33 feet. It would then be compressed to one half gallon in size (half its volume). When you returned the bottle to the surface, it would return to its original volume of one gallon.

Air Embolism

The air in your lungs responds the same way as the air in the plastic bottle. For a "skin diver" (no scuba), this is not a problem. When a skin diver holds his breath and swims underwater, the air in his lungs compresses. When he returns to the surface, the air expands back to its original volume. Since he doesn't take in any air while submerged, there is not any danger of overexpansion during ascent.

For scuba divers, however, an extremely hazardous condition can occur. If a diver at 33 feet filled his lungs to capacity, held his breath, and then swam to the surface, the air in his lungs would double in volume ($P^- = V^+$) and he would cause the rupture of the small air sacks in the lungs. This injury is called an *air embolism*.

You get an air embolism from holding your breath during an ascent. So, remember this rule: NEVER HOLD YOUR BREATH WHILE USING SCUBA DIVING EQUIPMENT.

Embolisms usually happen when a diver panics, and bolts for the surface holding his breath. If you have to make an emergency ascent, remember to exhale all the way to the surface. See Chapter 6 for more information on emergency ascents.

Equalizing

Your ears are affected by pressure changes. As you descend, the increasing pressure starts to push your eardrum inward. The remedy is to equalize your ears by forcing air into the middle ear. You do this by holding your nose and gently blowing against the resistance. This forces air up the Eustachian tube into the middle ear where it pushes against the eardrum being pushed in by outside water pressure. Your ears are equalized when the air pressure inside the ear is equal to the outside water pressure.

If you were to descend without equalizing your ears, you would risk rupturing your eardrum. The key to equalizing is to start before you feel discomfort in the ear. When you begin your descent, you should start to equalize as soon as your head is underwater. If you feel pain, do not descend any farther until you have fully equalized. If you're having difficulty equalizing, try ascending a few feet till the discomfort goes away. Now slowly descend, equalizing as you go. If you feel discomfort, you've waited too long before you started to equalize. Begin equalizing at the surface as soon as you begin your descent.

When you ascend, the air you have forced into your middle ear to equalize starts to expand ($P^- = V^+$). If your Eustachian tube has closed during the dive, the expanding air has no escape. This is called a reverse block. If it does not correct itself, as you ascend the expanding air will cause damage to your eardrum.

Reverse blocks usually only happen if you are diving with a cold or using a decongestant that wears off during the dive. The moral of the story is: Do not dive if you're sick or not feeling well.

Vertigo

When you ascend, the air in your middle ear starts to expand ($P^- = V^+$). If you ascend too rapidly you may experience vertigo (dizziness). This is one reason for a slow ascent and a pause before surfacing: this gives expanding air in your middle ear time to equalize.

If you do experience vertigo during an ascent, stop for a moment until it passes. In fact, any time you feel vertigo underwater you should stop what you're doing until it passes. It is a mistake to try ascending when dizzy, for three reasons. Your sense of which way is up may be wrong, you will have difficulty controlling your rate of ascent, and you may not be sure you have a clear path to the surface.

Another cause of vertigo could be a ruptured eardrum. This could happen if you continued to descend even if you were unable to equalize. Eventually the outside water pressure would become so great it would rupture the eardrum. The cold water rushing into the middle ear is painful and you will feel vertigo until the water in the ear has warmed to body temperature.

Mask Squeeze

The air space inside your mask is another area that is compressed by water pressure. As you descend, the volume of air inside your mask decreases. This causes the face plate of your mask to move closer to your face. The remedy is to exhale out of your nose. This restores the air volume and pushes the face plate back to its normal position.

Occasionally, the air space inside a mask will become so compressed that it will rupture blood vessels around the eye. If your eyes are bloodshot after a dive, you probably failed to equalize the air space inside your mask during the descent. This condition looks frightening, but passes after a few days.

New divers are the most prone to mask squeeze. They become so engrossed in the new experience of being underwater, they do not notice their nose being pressed up against the face plate of their mask!

ARCHIMEDES' PRINCIPLE

Archimedes' Principle has to do with buoyancy—the reason objects float or sink. It states: An object's buoyancy is directly related to the weight of the water it displaces. If an object weighs more than the water it displaces, it is negatively buoyant. If it weighs the same, it is neutrally buoyant. If it weighs less than the water it displaces, it is positively buoyant.

Here are some examples of Archimedes' Principle relating to diving.

1. A diver wearing a wetsuit is so buoyant that weights are needed in order to submerge. Why? The wetsuit increases the amount of water the diver displaces without adding much weight. The diver now weighs a lot less than the water he is displacing.

2. As a diver descends the wetsuit compresses. This decreases the amount of water the diver is displacing without changing the diver's weight, making the diver more negatively buoyant. To stop the descent, the diver must put some air into the BC. This increases the amount of water the diver is displacing without adding any appreciable weight. When the diver's weight equals the water he is displacing, he will neither sink nor rise. If the diver continues to add air to the BC, he will eventually weigh less than the water he is displacing and begin to rise.

3. Imagine a diver, neutrally buoyant in 40 feet of water. Now when that diver starts his ascent, what happens? His wetsuit will expand; as will the air in his BC, making him positively buoyant. If he couldn't control his buoyancy (by letting air out of the BC) his ascent would become dangerously fast and out of control.

✦ AIR

The air we breathe is made from a mixture of gases, oxygen, nitrogen, and carbon dioxide being the most important. Oxygen makes up 21% of the mixture, nitrogen 78%, and a variety of other gases make up the last 1%. (These are approximate figures.)

Oxygen is what our body needs to survive; our lungs pass oxygen from the air we breathe into our bloodstream. Nitrogen is not used by our bodies, but also passes into our bloodstream. Carbon dioxide is a by-product of consumed oxygen. Our body takes in oxygen, which is burned for fuel, and releases the waste product carbon dioxide.

To realize the possible dangers of breathing nitrogen under pressure, you need to understand two laws.

A basic understanding of the theory involved in diving is necessary to avoid injury while using compressed air.

➤ DALTON'S LAW

Dalton's Law states: The total pressure exerted by a gas is made up from the sum of all the contributing gases.

Dalton's Law is used to show that as you descend, the mixture of gases in the air stays the same, roughly 80% nitrogen and 20% oxygen. Although at 33 feet there is twice as much nitrogen and twice as much oxygen (see Boyle's Law), and at 99 feet there is four times as much, the percentages still stay the same; it is approximately an 80% nitrogen, 20% oxygen mixture.

The point is the deeper you go, the more nitrogen and oxygen you are breathing, but the mixture you're breathing is still roughly 80% nitrogen and 20% oxygen.

➤ HENRY'S LAW

Henry's Law states: The amount of gas that can be dissolved in a liquid is related to how much pressure it is under.

To visualize Henry's Law, imagine a bottle of soda water. When you look at the bottle with the cap on, you cannot see any gas bubbles in the liquid (because the gas is under pressure). When you take the cap off, you release the pressure, and can see the gas bubbles in the liquid.

The Bends

When you are diving, your body behaves like the bottle of soda; your blood is the liquid and nitrogen is the gas we are most concerned with. As you descend, the pressure increases and your blood absorbs more nitrogen. The deeper you go, the faster it happens, since you are under greater pressure and you are breathing more air. Remember from Boyle's Law, it takes *four times* as much air to fill your lungs at 99 feet as it does at the surface.

When you ascend, it is like taking the cap off the bottle: pressure is released and the nitrogen returns to gas form. This is when the potential problems can occur.

If the gas bubbles are too big they will block arteries. A minor blockage might cause pain in your joints; a more severe block could cause a stroke or heart attack! This congestion is called THE BENDS, or DECOMPRESSION SICKNESS.

To avoid getting bent, divers refer to charts called the DIVE TABLES. The Dive Tables tell you how long you can stay at various depths without undue risk of decompression sickness.

The Tables provide information so you can ascend before your body has absorbed an amount of nitrogen that would make surfacing potentially dangerous. This amount of time you can stay down is referred to as the No-Decompression Time.

The deeper you are, the shorter the no-decompression times are. For example, according to the U.S. Navy Tables the no-decompression time at 40 feet is 200 minutes; at 100 feet it's twenty-five minutes. That's because at 100 feet you're under four times as much pressure, and are breathing four times as much nitrogen (Boyle's Law). The nitrogen is being absorbed into your blood at a faster rate because of the greater partial pressure (Henry's Law), so you have less no-decompression time at 100 feet than at 40 feet.

(Different organizations put out different tables. The U.S. Navy Dive Tables are not the same as NAUI's. The important thing to remember here is to use the same tables when working out a dive schedule. *Never* switch back and forth between tables during dives on the same day.)

Diving at Altitudes Above Sea Level

The Dive Tables are based on returning to 1 atm (or 14.7 psi) of pressure after a dive. If you were diving in a lake at a higher altitude, the atmospheric pressure would be less. For instance, at 7,000 feet, the atmospheric pressure is about 11.34; at 12,000 feet it's about 9.349. The pressures are less at higher altitude because there is less atmosphere over your head.

The danger for divers is that the lower pressures will allow nitrogen bubbles in your blood to become larger than is safe, and you could get bent. There are specially modified Dive Tables for use at high altitude. If you're going to dive in a lake, find out what the altitude is, and use Dive Tables for that specific altitude.

Flying after Diving

If you're going to be traveling on an airplane, *you should not dive for at least twelve hours* before the flight. When you are in a small plane, the cabin is usually pressurized. Since you'd be at a higher elevation, nitrogen bubbles in your blood could expand beyond a safe size and you'd get bent.

With commercial airlines the cabins are pressurized, but not to 14.7 psi. So you still run the risk of being bent. If you have been doing a lot of deep diving or have been diving for several days in a row (such as on a vacation), it is recommended you wait twenty-four hours before flying.

Nitrogen Narcosis

Nitrogen Narcosis—also known as "Rapture of the Deep" —is another problem brought about from breathing large amounts of nitrogen under pressure. When a diver is under its effect, or "narced," the diver feels drunk, is lightheaded, and usually has a false sense of well-being.

The danger is that people's judgment usually deteriorates when they are narced. They forget to monitor their air, ignore depth limitations, and become fixated with useless tasks.

Nitrogen Narcosis usually is first noticed by aware divers between 60 and 100 feet. A diver may not have ever noticed being narced, and then one day get narced doing the same type of dive, depth, and activity. There are few hard and fast rules about nitrogen narcosis.

The remedy for nitrogen narcosis is to ascend until the effect is gone. There are no lasting effects, so you can continue the dive once you ascend to a depth where the narcosis passes.

Divers in cold water after doing their first deep dive often wonder why the water becomes warmer at greater depths. In reality the water became colder, but they thought it was warmer because they were mildly narced.

SOUND UNDERWATER

Sound travels four times faster in water than in air! Because sound travels so fast underwater it reaches both of your ears at almost the same time (as far as your brain is concerned), making it practically impossible to tell the direction a sound is coming from. This is one reason that if you hear a boat's engine while submerged, you should stay submerged until it's gone since you won't be able to tell what direction it's traveling in.

Another problem is signaling your buddy. Most divers bang something (such as their knife) against their tank to get their buddy's attention. While this will work if you're within sight of each other, it won't work if you're hidden behind a rock. For your buddy to be able to assist you in an emergency, you must be within sight of each other during the dive. This doesn't mean you must actually be looking at each other the whole time, but you should be close enough that if one of you should need help and signal by making the noise, the other diver will be able to locate you without searching.

HEAT UNDERWATER

Water absorbs heat *twenty-five times* faster than air. That means when you are in the water, you are losing body heat twenty-five times faster than when on land. Imagine standing outside in a pair of shorts and a light shirt when it's 65°F. outside; you would not be too uncomfortable. Now imagine jumping into 65°F. water in the same pair of shorts and shirt. Because water absorbs heat twenty-five times faster, you would be cold very quickly.

LIGHT UNDERWATER

Objects underwater appear to be *25% larger* when viewed through a mask. This magnification is caused by the refraction (bending) of light rays as they pass from one medium (water) to another (air). This can be confusing at first. I still think lobsters I catch somehow shrink on the trip to the surface.

Because water is denser than air, light is absorbed as it passes through it. Starting in about 15 feet, the red end of the color spectrum is lost. By 30 feet, all reds and oranges are absorbed. Greens and yellows are lost by 60 feet, and by 100 feet, everything takes on a bluish hue.

Color loss is one reason people often say the prettiest diving is in shallow water. Below 60 feet, even if something is really colorful, you cannot see the colors without an underwater light.

CHAPTER 6

Dive Tables

The dive tables tell you long you can stay underwater without getting decompression sickness (the bends). All dive classes teach students how to use the tables, but if you haven't used them in a while it's easy to forget how to work them. Some divers buy a computer as soon as they're certified, and so never have to use the tables. I believe in the use of dive computers, but I also think all divers should know how to work dive tables. The computers are machines and do break down occasionally!

Dive tables can vary slightly from one manufacturer to another. One set of tables may be more conservative than another, and it's not unusual to come across two sets of tables with different numbers, which can be confusing. So whose tables should you use? I recommend the U.S. Navy tables, or any of the tables put out by NAUI, SSI, or PADI—all of which are based on the U.S. Navy tables.

⚓ TERMINOLOGY

Understanding the terms used in association with the dive tables will make the tables easier to use. If you know, for example, that "Residual Nitrogen Time" refers to nitrogen that is left in your body from a previous dive, you'll have an easier time understanding why you have to take it into consideration when calculating repetitive dives. Here are some of the terms used with most dive tables.

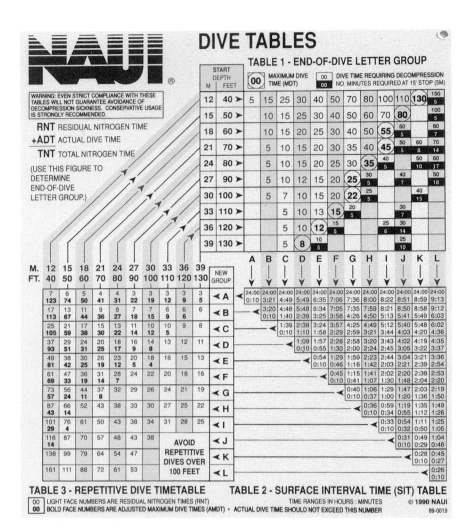

NON-REPETITIVE DIVE: Any dive made with at least a twenty-four hour interval since the last dive you made. If you have been diving within twenty-four hours of a dive you're about to make, you cannot calculate it as a non-repetitive dive.

REPETITIVE DIVE: Any dive made within twenty-four hours of a previous dive. For example: If you hadn't been diving all week and then went for a dive on Saturday morning, that dive would be a non-repetitive dive. If three hours after this dive you go for a second dive...the second dive is a repetitive dive since it is made within twenty-four hours of the last dive.

NO-DECOMPRESSION TIME (N.D.T.): This is the amount of time you can stay underwater without getting bent on a non-repetitive dive. If you have made a dive within twenty-four hours the no-decompression time must be adjusted because nitrogen from the previous dive must be taken into account.

RESIDUAL NITROGEN TIME (R.N.T.): This is the nitrogen left in your body from a previous dive. Any dive made within twenty-four hours of a previous dive is a repetitive dive because you have nitrogen in your body from the previous dive. This residual nitrogen is stated in minutes on the dive tables.

ADJUSTED NO-DECOMPRESSION TIME (A.N.D.T.): No-decompression time is adjusted by subtracting the residual nitrogen time. Remember that on any repetitive dive you have nitrogen left in your body from the previous dive. Your no-decompression time must be adjusted to take this nitrogen into account.

SURFACE INTERVAL (S.I.): This refers to the amount of time you spend out of the water between dives.

BOTTOM TIME (B.T.): The amount of time you actually spend submerged during a dive.

TOTAL BOTTOM TIME (T.B.T.): Bottom time and residual nitrogen time added together. You must always add the residual nitrogen time to your bottom time on a repetitive dive. This is important and is the step most people forget to do.

GROUP LETTER: A letter of the alphabet is used on the dive tables to symbolize the amount of nitrogen you have in your body.

✦ USING THE DIVE TABLES

A set of NAUI'S dive tables are used to illustrate the following text. You may want to buy a set from your local dive shop to aid you in following along. (Note: NAUI'S terminology and method of using the tables is slightly different than mine. Their dive tables are pictured here for the purpose of illustration only.)

Dive tables are referred to as a set because they are made up of three charts, or tables. Table 1 tells you what the no-decompression times are for various depths. Table 2 is used after your surface interval, since your body releases nitrogen while you are out of the water. Table 3 is used to calculate how long you can stay submerged on a repetitive dive.

		A	B	C	D	E	F	G	H	I	J	K
15	50 ➤		10	15	25	30	40	50	60	70	(80)		10/5
18	60 ➤		10	15	20	25	30	40	50	(55)	60/5		8/7
21	70 ➤		5	10	15	20	30	35	40	(45)	50/5	60/8	7/1
24	80 ➤		5	10	15	20	25	30	(35)	40/5		50/10	6/1
27	90 ➤		5	10	12	15	20	(25)	30/5		40/7		5/1
30	100 ➤		5	7	10	15	20	(22)	25/5		40/15		
33	110 ➤			5	10	13	(15)	20/5		30/7			
36	120 ➤			5	10	(12)	15/5			25/6	30/14		
39	130 ➤			5	(8)	10/5					25/10		

Table 1

The diagram in Figure 1 is the work area you will use to fill in the various bits of information needed when working the dive tables. We will fill this out as we go through sample dives.

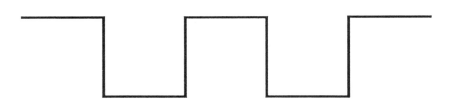

Figure 1

The First Dive

The first thing you need to decide before you go diving is: How deep will you be going? Figure out what your maximum

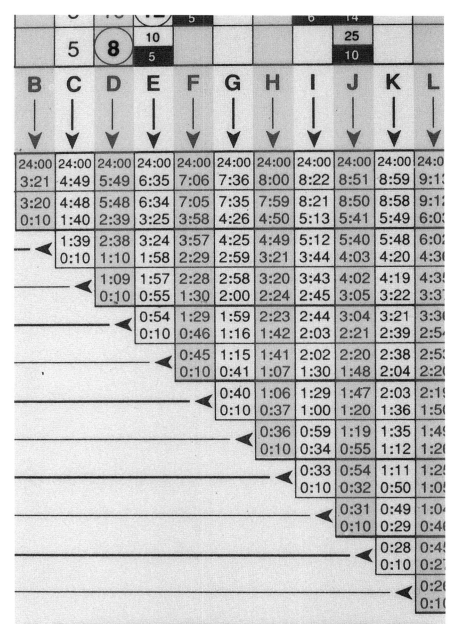

5	(8)	10						25	
		5						10	

B	C	D	E	F	G	H	I	J	K	L
24:00	24:00	24:00	24:00	24:00	24:00	24:00	24:00	24:00	24:00	24:0
3:21	4:49	5:49	6:35	7:06	7:36	8:00	8:22	8:51	8:59	9:1:
3:20	4:48	5:48	6:34	7:05	7:35	7:59	8:21	8:50	8:58	9:1:
0:10	1:40	2:39	3:25	3:58	4:26	4:50	5:13	5:41	5:49	6:0:
	1:39	2:38	3:24	3:57	4:25	4:49	5:12	5:40	5:48	6:0:
	0:10	1:10	1:58	2:29	2:59	3:21	3:44	4:03	4:20	4:3(
		1:09	1:57	2:28	2:58	3:20	3:43	4:02	4:19	4:3!
		0:10	0:55	1:30	2:00	2:24	2:45	3:05	3:22	3:3'
			0:54	1:29	1:59	2:23	2:44	3:04	3:21	3:3(
			0:10	0:46	1:16	1:42	2:03	2:21	2:39	2:5-
				0:45	1:15	1:41	2:02	2:20	2:38	2:5:
				0:10	0:41	1:07	1:30	1:48	2:04	2:2(
					0:40	1:06	1:29	1:47	2:03	2:1!
					0:10	0:37	1:00	1:20	1:36	1:5(
						0:36	0:59	1:19	1:35	1:4!
						0:10	0:34	0:55	1:12	1:2(
							0:33	0:54	1:11	1:2!
							0:10	0:32	0:50	1:0!
								0:31	0:49	1:0-
								0:10	0:29	0:4(
									0:28	0:4!
									0:10	0:2'
										0:2(
										0:1(

2 - SURFACE INTERVAL TIME (SIT) TABL

TIME RANGES IN HOURS : MINUTES   © 1990 NA|

Table 2

								33	110
								36	120
								39	130

12 / 40	15 / 50	18 / 60	21 / 70	24 / 80	27 / 90	30 / 100	33 / 110	36 / 120	39 / 130	NEW GROUP
7 / 123	6 / 74	5 / 50	4 / 41	4 / 31	3 / 22	3 / 19	3 / 12	3 / 9	3 / 5	◄ A
17 / 113	13 / 67	11 / 44	9 / 36	8 / 27	7 / 18	7 / 15	6 / 9	6 / 6	6	◄ B
25 / 105	21 / 59	17 / 38	15 / 30	13 / 22	11 / 14	10 / 12	10 / 5	9	8	◄ C
37 / 93	29 / 51	24 / 31	20 / 25	18 / 17	16 / 9	14 / 8	13	12	11	◄ D
49 / 81	38 / 42	30 / 25	26 / 19	23 / 12	20 / 5	18 / 4	16	15	13	◄ E
61 / 69	47 / 33	36 / 19	31 / 14	28 / 7	24	22	20	18	16	◄ F
73 / 57	56 / 24	44 / 11	37 / 8	32	29	26	24	21	19	◄ G
87 / 43	66 / 14	52	43	38	33	30	27	25	22	◄ H
101 / 29	76 / 4	61	50	43	38	34	31	28	25	◄ I
116 / 14	87	70	57	48	43	38	AVOID ↗ REPETITIVE DIVES OVER 100 FEET			◄ J
138	99	79	64	54	47					◄ K
161	111	88	72	61	53					◄ L

Table 3

depth will be and write it on your chart in the area shown in Figure 2. In this example the maximum depth is 100 feet.

Whatever depth you decide on, YOU CANNOT EXCEED IT DURING THE DIVE. For this reason you may want to calculate for a greater depth than the one you are planning.

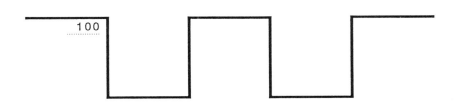

Figure 2

This way if you do want to go deeper during the dive you'll have a little leeway.

If the depth you're going to is in between the depths written on the dive tables, enter the table at the greater depth. In this case, let's says you are boat diving and the boat is anchored in 91 feet of water. You cannot calculate for 90 feet even though 91 is closer to 90 than 100. You must call it a dive to 100 feet.

The next thing you need to know is how long you can stay submerged. We will assume this is the first dive within a

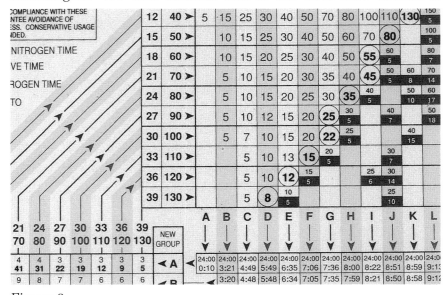

Figure 3

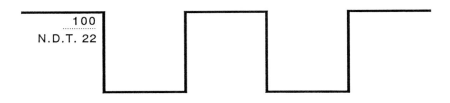

Figure 4

twenty-four hour period, so you need to know what the no-decompression time is for the deepest depth you're planning to go to. Look to Table 1 for this information.

Depth is listed in a vertical line at the top of the dive tables. It's written in both meters and feet. (See Figure 3.) Go down the column until you get to 100 feet and then travel to the right until you get to a number in a circle. That is your maximum dive time (MDT). At 100 feet it's 22: this is the no-decompression time. So, at 100 feet the no-decompression time is twenty-two minutes. However, you should never dive the tables to their outer limits. If the tables say you can stay twenty-two minutes, for example, I recommend you cut a few minutes off the time to give yourself a safety margin.

Enter the no-decompression time on your chart as shown in Figure 4.

If you are only doing one dive within a twenty-four hour period then you're done. Once you know the no-decompression time for the depth you're going to, you can go diving. If, however, you want to do a second dive, more calculations are necessary.

The Second Dive

Most textbooks define bottom time as the length of time from beginning your descent to beginning your direct ascent to the surface. I think it's easier and safer to define your bottom time as *all* the time you're underwater. Let's say our bottom time on the last dive was eighteen minutes. Enter a bottom time of eighteen minutes on your chart, as shown in Figure 5.

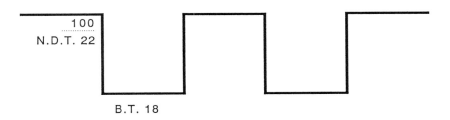

Figure 5

After a dive we have nitrogen in our bodies. The dive tables use letters from the alphabet to symbolize this amount of nitrogen. To figure out our group letter for this dive, travel to the right of 100 feet on Table 1 until you get to your bottom time. In our example it's twenty minutes.

Since our bottom time of eighteen minutes is in between fifteen and twenty, the greater time must be used. *Always* go to the next greater time if your bottom time is in between the times listed on the tables.

From twenty minutes travel down until you come to the group letter F. (see Figure 6.)

Enter the letter F on your chart as shown in Figure 7.

Let's say that after your dive you have lunch and get your tank filled while the boat is moved to another site. By the time you're ready to go back in the water, two hours and forty-five minutes have passed, written as 2:45 minutes in diving lingo. This is your surface interval time. Enter the surface interval time on your chart as shown in Figure 8.

Your body has been releasing nitrogen during your surface interval. This means you're no longer an F diver. To acquire your new group letter, travel down from the letter F on Table 2 until you get to a time that your surface interval 2:45 minutes is in between. In this example it's the box with 2:29 and 3:57 written in it. (See Figure 9.)

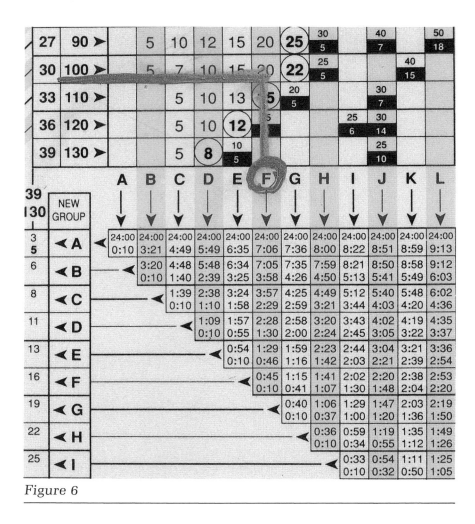

Figure 6

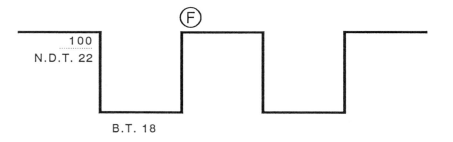

Figure 7

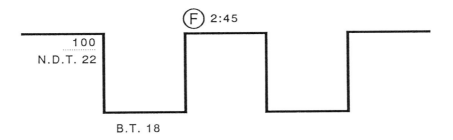

Figure 8

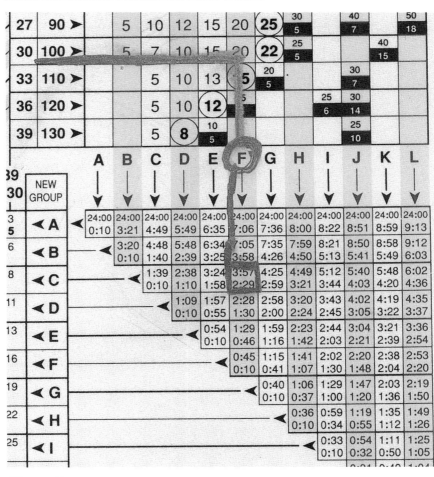

Figure 9

40	50	60	70	80	90	100	110	120	130	GROUP
7 / 23	6 / 74	5 / 50	4 / 41	4 / 31	3 / 22	3 / 19	3 / 12	3 / 9	3 / 5	◄A
17 / 13	13 / 67	11 / 44	9 / 36	8 / 27	7 / 18	7 / 15	6 / 9	6 / 6	6	◄B
25 / 05	21 / 59	17 / 38	15 / 30	13 / 22	11 / 14	10 / 12	10 / 5	9	8	◄C
37 / 93	29 / 51	24 / 31	20 / 25	18 / 17	16 / 9	14 / 8	13	12	11	◄D
49 / 31	38 / 42	30 / 25	26 / 19	23 / 12	20 / 5	18 / 4	16	15	13	◄E
61 / 69	47 / 33	36 / 19	31 / 14	28 / 7	24	22	20	18	16	◄F
73 / 57	56 / 24	44 / 11	37 / 8	32	29	26	24	21	19	◄G
87 / 43	66 / 14	52	43	38	33	30	27	25	22	◄H
01 / 29	76 / 4	61	50	43	38	34	31	28	25	◄I
16 / 14	87	70	57	48	43	38	AVOID REPETITIVE DIVES OVER 100 FEET			◄J
38	99	79	64	54	47					◄K
61	111	88	72	61	53					◄L

Figure 9A

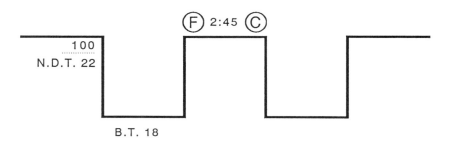

Figure 10

Now travel to the left until you get to your new group letter, which in this case is C. (See Figure 9A.) Enter your new group letter on your chart as shown in Figure 10.

You now need to decide what your maximum depth will be on the dive you're about to do. Let's say it's 80 feet. Enter 80 feet and the no-decompression time for 80 feet on your chart exactly like you did before (see Figure 11). You should remember how to get the no-decompression time from our earlier example for 100 feet.

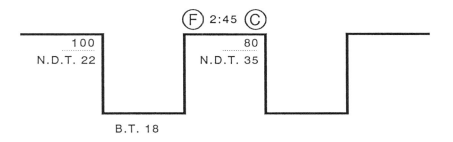

Figure 11

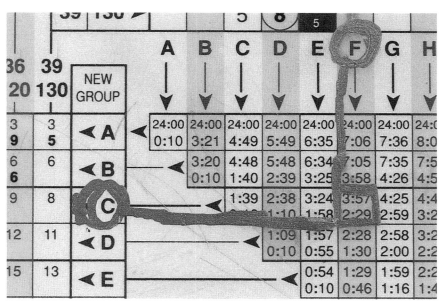

Figure 12

Since you have nitrogen in your body from a previous dive, you have to recalculate your no-decompression time. To do this find the box where your depth (80 feet) and your group letter (C) meet on Table 3. In this example it's the box with 13 and 22 in it. (See Figure 12.)

The top number is your residual nitrogen time and the bottom number is the adjusted no-decompression time.

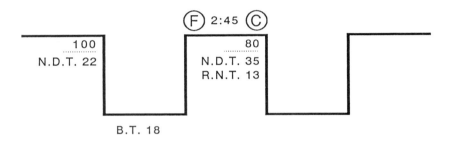

Figure 13

Enter the residual nitrogen time on your chart as shown in Figure 13. Now subtract the residual nitrogen time from the no-decompression time as shown in Figure 14. This gives you the adjusted no-decompression time of twenty-two minutes. Table 3 on the dive tables does this calculation for you, but writing it out this way will help you understand how these numbers relate to each other.

In this example you could go to 80 feet for twenty-two minutes. If you were to go to 80 feet for the non-adjusted no-decompression time of thirty-five minutes you would get bent. On repetitive dives you must always subtract the residual nitrogen time from the no-decompression time to get the adjusted no-decompression time.

Enter the residual nitrogen time on your chart as shown in Figure 15. At the end of your dive you will need to add your bottom time to the residual nitrogen time. It's as if you have spent thirteen minutes (the residual nitrogen time) submerged before you begin your dive. Some divers think of residual nitrogen time as "penalty time."

The adjusted no-decompression time in this example is

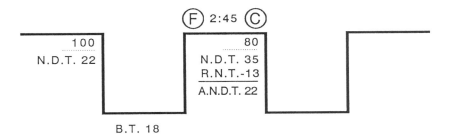

Figure 14

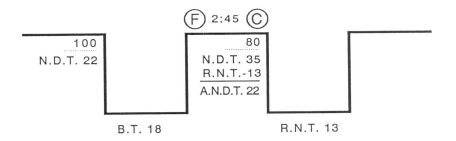

Figure 15

twenty-two minutes. But not wanting to dive the tables to the limits we surface after seventeen minutes. Enter the bottom time of seventeen minutes on your chart as shown in Figure 16.

Now add the bottom time and the residual nitrogen time. This give you the total bottom time of thirty minutes. (See Figure 17.)

Use the total bottom time to re-enter the tables at the top to get a new group letter. In this example 80 feet for thirty minutes makes us a G diver. Enter the letter G on your chart as shown in Figure 18.

If you were going to do another dive you would calculate as described above. After your surface interval, figure out

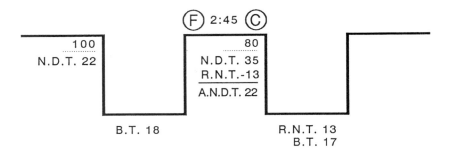

Figure 16

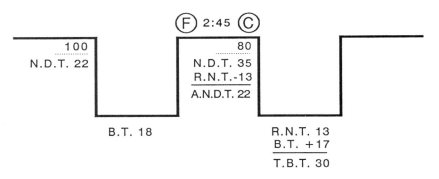

Figure 17

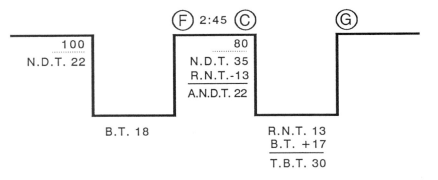

Figure 18

what your new group letter is and keep going to calculate your adjusted no-decompression time.

Always remember that for your dive not to be considered a repetitive dive you have to be out of the water for twenty-four hours or longer.

Planning Your Surface Interval

Often during a day of diving you'll know in advance how deep your next dive is going to be and how much time you want to spend at that depth. If you're going to be doing a repetitive dive the question becomes: How long do you have to stay out of the water before you can make the desired dive?

To answer that, first figure out what your group letter is at the end of your last dive. Let's say you're an F diver and you know you want to go to 80 feet for at least eighteen minutes on your next dive. Look at Table 3 of the dive tables and travel down the 80-foot column until you get to a box that has eighteen or a higher number in the bottom of the box. In this example it's twenty-two. Now travel to the right over to Table 2 until you get to the times box that is under your group letter (F). In this example it's the box with 3:57 and 2:29 written in it. This tells you that a Surface Interval of 2:29 minutes would be needed before the desired dive to 80 feet for eighteen minutes could be made.

A diver crawls out of the surf after being knocked down. Remember to keep all gear on and in place while you are in the water.

CHAPTER 7

Self-Sufficient Diver

Self-sufficient diver is a term I use to describe a diver who is capable of solving any problems that may arise underwater —without the assistance of a buddy. A lot of emphasis is put on the "buddy system" in most contemporary scuba classes, which occasionally creates divers who then look to their diving partners—rather than themselves—when they get in trouble. That is not to say that it is perfectly safe for you to dive alone, but you should be capable of handling any emergency by yourself without looking for your buddy first.

An out-of-air emergency is a good example. Many divers' first instinct when they run out of air is to locate their buddy. Locating the buddy may take a few seconds; swimming to the buddy also takes time. More time may be lost trying to communicate with a diver who doesn't understand what is happening or doesn't have the proper skills to respond.

Avoiding out-of-air emergencies is part of being a self-sufficient diver, but for the sake of conversation, let's say you've run out of air in 100 feet of water, and your buddy is 60 feet away. As a self-sufficient diver, you have two options: 1. You can make a free swimming ascent without dropping your weights. 2. You could drop your weight belt and make a buoyant ascent.

A self-sufficient diver uses those few moments that would have been spent searching and reaching a buddy to resolve the situation himself *before* his lack of air becomes critical.

This chapter contains the essence of what you need to know and practice to become self-sufficient in the water.

⚓ WEAR YOUR MASK—SOMETHING IN YOUR MOUTH

This sounds exceedingly simple, but you'd be surprised at how many people take their masks off, especially when on the surface! Often when I rescue people on the surface, one of the main causes of their anxiety is water splashing in their faces. Some places—such as California's Channel Islands—can have rough surface conditions caused by wind or chop. Add to that the fact that the diver is tired, and may be confronted by a long swim back to the boat or shore, and you have the beginnings of a potential problem!

Usually the diver in the above paragraph not only isn't wearing his mask, but he doesn't have his regulator or snorkel in his mouth. This person now is not only having trouble seeing because of the water splashing around him, he's also having trouble keeping his head above the water. When I reach him he tells me, "I can't breathe, I'm sinking, I think I'm drowning!" If this diver: 1. had his mask on, 2. had his regulator in his mouth, and 3. had established positive buoyancy, there would be no problem.

You may have been taught or told that it's wrong to use your regulator while swimming on the surface. Unfortunately some instructors mistakenly believe that the regulator is only to be used underwater, while the snorkel must be used on the surface. They are incorrect.

It's not uncommon for beach divers to do their entries and exits through some kind of surf. I know from personal experience that some people feel more comfortable going through the surf with their regulators. Imagine being knocked over by a wave and being held face down against the sand for a few moments by a passing wave. If you have your regulator in your mouth, and your mask on, you can see and you can breathe...you don't have a problem. The same diver with nothing in his mouth and his mask on his forehead...may have a problem.

Another example is entering the water from a boat. A friend of mine recently "giant striated" off a boat with his snorkel in his mouth. When he hit the water, the water movement combined with the motion of the boat pulled him under the boat. While he was groping to find his regulator, he was hit on the head by the rocking boat and inhaled water. Fortunately, a fellow diver saw what was happening, jumped in the water, and pulled him clear of the boat. Needless to say, my friend now enters the water with his regulator in his mouth.

Now before you go to throw your snorkel into the surf line, never to use it again, realize it is a useful and essential tool—and all divers should have one. But don't feel that you must always use it on the surface if you feel more comfortable and safer using your regulator.

WEIGHT BELTS ARE DISPOSABLE

This also seems obvious, but it continually surprises me how many divers are reluctant to dispose of their weights in anything less than a full-blown, life-threatening emergency!

I've dropped my weight belt on a couple of occasions while swimming on the surface when I realized conditions were getting rough and/or I was becoming fatigued. The thinking here is to resolve problems before they occur.

Imagine surfacing after a long beach dive to find the surf has increased. Dropping your weight belt might make your exit through the surf easier.

Recently while diving in the frigid waters of Lake Superior, a friend of mine almost drowned on the surface, only 40 feet from the boat. At the end of her dive she discovered her power inflator had malfunctioned. While attempting to inflate her BC manually, she had to struggle to keep her head above water. Add to the scenario that she had begun to lose manual dexterity due to the extreme cold, and you have the beginnings of a problem.

When we talked about the above scenario, I asked her why she hadn't dropped her weight belt. Her reply was, "It wasn't an emergency."

In reality, if she hadn't been pulled out of the water by two fellow divers, she might have drowned.

When people die while diving, it's usually the result of a lot of little problems. Dropping your weight belt may solve one problem before it becomes an emergency. Try to solve little problems as they arise, rather than letting them pile up until you really are in the middle of an emergency.

COMFORT LEVEL

To dive within your comfort level means simply not to do dives that make you feel uncomfortable. If during a dive you feel anxious or nervous, the dive may be exceeding your comfort level. It is important to know where your comfort level is and not exceed it. In other words, if you've never been diving below 60 feet and your dive buddy wants to do a dive to 150 feet, making that dive would most likely exceed your comfort level.

You can increase your comfort level by educating yourself about the things that make you feel apprehensive. If you are uncomfortable with deep diving for example, rather than doing one dive where you exceed your comfort level, you could do a series of dives over a few weeks that get progressively deeper. Another example would be someone's first dive through large surf. By first doing a couple of skin diving entries, he would gain some experience with the surf before going in with the added weight of a tank and weight belt.

Anytime you feel apprehensive prior to or during a dive — stop and think about whether you are exceeding (or are about to exceed) your comfort level. If you are, don't do the dive (or stop what you are doing) until you receive competent instruction or educate yourself about what you fear.

ADJUSTING EQUIPMENT

Adjust all equipment prior to entering the water. In fact, adjust it before you even get to the water. Often I see divers who — just prior to jumping in the water — suddenly decide their fins are too loose or the weights on their weight belt are not properly adjusted or some other piece of equipment is malfunctioning. The added stress of fumbling with your gear moments before you jump in the water is not conducive to a relaxed and safe diving experience.

Take some time to thoroughly check all of your equipment the night before you go diving. Weight belts in particular are often an overlooked item. Use weight belt keepers (a device that keeps the weight in position on the belt) to prevent the weights from sliding around on the belt during the dive. Have you ever gone to put your weight belt on, only to discover that the weights have moved and that it is now impossible to tighten the belt completely? Weight belt keepers prevent this. You can also hold weights in place by putting a half turn twist in the weight belt as you lace the weight on.

Make sure that weights are distributed evenly on your hips; weights that sit in the small of your back will be pressed upon by your tank, which is uncomfortable.

I'd also recommend that you use (if possible) two large weights rather than a pile of small ones. If you use 22 pounds of lead for example, an 11 pound weight on each hip is simpler than two 5's and six 2's. The more you can streamline your weight belt, the better.

Gauges are another piece of equipment that novice divers tend to strap all over themselves. Rather than have your SPG on a hose, a depth gauge strapped to your wrist, and a watch and compass on your other wrist, mount all gauges in one unit at the end of your SPG hose. Having your gauges mounted all over the place makes it difficult to obtain vital information at a glance. Having all of your gauges mounted in one console allows you to see how much air you have, how deep you are, directional information, and how long you have been there—all at a glance!

Many manufacturers make complete consoles specifically for this purpose. Penform is a company that makes custom consoles so you can fit any imaginable selection of gauges you wish. A typical custom made, three-gauge console costs about $40. This of course does not include the cost of the gauges.

Using a computer is another solution, since they supply all of the above information and much more. (See Chapter 15 for more information about computers.)

➤ BUY A COMPASS

Knowing where you are underwater in relation to your exit point (be it shore or boat) will make you a lot more secure and confident while diving. It is surprising how many divers don't use a compass and simply swim around until they are low on air—at which point they surface and look for the boat!

Swimming back to the boat or shore underwater is a lot less stressful than doing it on the surface. When diving from a boat for example, I like to always begin and end my dives at the anchor line.

I use and recommend Ikelite's compass (model 2500) for a couple of reasons. First, it can be worn on your wrist (if you insist) but also fits in a variety of consoles. Also, it is easy to use. The compass dial has a white arrow on it and the bezel has two white slashes on it. You simply point your console (with the compass on the end) and turn the bezel until the white slashes are on either side of the arrow on the compass dial. Now once you want to re-establish direction, you move the compass around until the arrow once again is aligned with the slashes.

Another feature I like is that opposite the white arrow on the compass dial is a black arrow; this simplifies 180° turns (going back the way you came) since all you have to do is line the black arrow up with the white slashes.

Underwater navigational aids should be used in connection with your compass. Off most beaches for example, there are ripples in the sand that run parallel to shore. So if you are swimming across the ripples, you are probably swimming towards shore or swimming out to sea. Pressure felt from depth changes can also be used for directional control. If you

If you're doing deep dives it's a good idea to have a hang-off tank waiting in case you return low on air. This way you will always be able to do a long safety stop.

have to equalize your ears every few moments, then you are obviously getting deeper. Examination of the underwater terrain where you dive will probably reveal other navigational aids you can use.

✦ BUOYANCY CONTROL

Buoyancy control is possibly one of the most overlooked (and easiest) skills needed to be comfortable in the water. Mastering buoyancy control will enable you to be neutrally buoyant throughout your dive. This frees you from having to "think" about your buoyancy, thus enabling you to focus fully on the dive. For example, let's say your buddy accidentally kicks your mask, flooding it with water. Clearing a mask isn't difficult. But clearing a mask while drifting towards the surface might cause anxiety since the diver now has *two* problems to solve.

Mastering buoyancy control will make you more confident in the water. Here is an exercise that you can do to practice achieving neutral buoyancy. While underwater get in a position (while negatively buoyant) to do a push-up on your knees. After each push-up add a little air to your BC. Keep doing this until you are able to "hang" off the bottom with your knees *gently* touching. With a little practice you will be able to achieve neutral buoyancy quickly at any depth while diving.

✦ CONTINUED EDUCATION

I've been diving over seventeen years and I still annually attend seminars and workshops. Continuing your education ensures that your skills and technical knowledge stay current. For instance, there are still divers out there who don't know anything about alternate air supplies. While they may not necessarily be at risk because of their lack of knowledge, they would unquestionably have a higher margin of safety if they knew about this piece of equipment that many of us consider mandatory.

Take some time to read about what's going on in the sport diving field and take an occasional seminar, workshop, or advanced dive course!

⌁ STAY ACTIVE

I am referring to staying active as a diver! If you haven't been diving in six months and you decide to go on a beach dive in 4-foot surf, you could conceivably have a problem since your skills may be a bit rusty. I personally define "active" as a minimum of one dive per month. Experienced divers (more than fifty dives logged) could probably let more time lapse between dives. I don't think anyone, however, could consider himself an "active" diver if more than six months has passed without doing a dive.

Due to location or other reasons, some people do not and cannot go diving over a long period of time. If you haven't been diving for a long time, don't assume you can pick up at the level where you left off. Gradually reaccustom yourself to deeper and more difficult dives.

⌁ BE A THINKING DIVER

Just about every problem you could conceivably encounter while diving can be resolved by you with a little thought. Being a thinking diver means that you keep your brain turned on before, during, and after the dive. If, while diving a diver unexpectedly discovers a cave, enters it, gets lost, runs out of air, and dies—he wasn't thinking. Minimal thought would have told this person that entering the cave was a bad idea since he didn't have adequate training or equipment.

Think about solutions to possible problems before they happen. What will you do if you run out of air? What will you do if your BC power inflator fails? What would you do if you saw a great white shark? What would you do if both legs cramped and you were unable to swim? How about if you needed to signal shore from a mile away? The point is, let your imagination run wild and dream up as many scenarios as you can—and then search for the solutions. Having a predetermined plan of attack in an emergency may make the difference between doing nothing, doing the wrong thing, or quickly and simply resolving the situation.

If you encounter problems you didn't expect while diving —don't panic. Stop what you are doing and look for a solution. Imagine a diver in 100 feet of water who suddenly discovers his submersible pressure gauge has stopped working!

I actually know of a case of this happening where the diver took "a guess" at how much air he had left and continued his dive. Unfortunately, his calculations were off and he ran out of air in 100 feet of water and had to make an emergency ascent. In his panicked state he swallowed enough salt water to supply a small aquarium.

Some years ago while diving in the Cayman Islands I encountered a situation: The dive guide told our group that the first dive would be to 100 feet. Twenty-one minutes into the dive, I began to wonder when we would be surfacing since the no-decompression time for 100 feet is twenty-five minutes (according to the U.S. Navy Dive Tables). The real shock came when the guide led the group below 100 feet—exceeding the no-decompression limits. Deciding the guide had just become a safety hazard, I surfaced, making a 10-foot safety spot on the way. A few minutes later, the rest of the group surfaced. When I expressed my concerns, our guide answered, "Don't worry about it. We were only there for a couple of minutes."

The moral of this story is do not rely on other people to make you safe; you are responsible for your safety. (The above story took place before computers hit the market and also was not based on a multilevel dive profile. I do realize that both computers and multilevel profiles are used by today's dive guides and are safe practices.)

Diving is a physical sport, but being safe in the water relies as heavily on brain power as it does on physical skills.

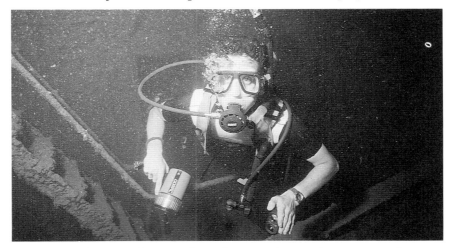

It's easy to become lost inside a shipwreck. Don't enter wrecks, caves, or any other overhead environment without first obtaining qualified instruction.

CHAPTER 8

Emergency Procedures and First Aid

Diving is an extremely safe sport. When problems do occur, it's almost always due to the person doing something they already knew they *shouldn't* have done. Or from someone going diving without first obtaining the proper instruction. An example of this would be someone who gets caught in an underwater cave, runs out of air, and drowns.

It would be beyond the scope of this book to include an in-depth explanation of every type of diving accident possible. What follows is a discussion of the most common types of situations you may encounter.

Most diving emergencies, whether they be small or large, involve some form of diver stress. Diver stress in itself has often led to divers getting into trouble.

➤ THE CAUSES OF DIVER'S STRESS

Equipment is often one overlooked cause of diver's stress. For example, something as simple as your mask fogging up can cause apprehension because you can't see. This is one reason I highly recommend you defog your mask before going diving, using the commercially available products or even toothpaste.

Another problem new divers often encounter is an improperly fitting wetsuit. A constrictive wetsuit can make breathing difficult. Students using rental gear may be more prone to encountering this problem.

Improper buoyancy control may also be a cause of stress. Buoyancy problems can be caused by too much or too little weight on your weight belt. Take some time to do a buoyancy check and get your weight belt properly adjusted. An unfamiliar BC or power inflator can cause buoyancy problems. For example, a full game bag is going to change your buoyancy, and the power inflator is the only way to compensate (other than dropping the bag). It is important not only to have your equipment completely adjusted for comfortable fit, but also to become comfortable in using it through practice.

Practice working with your gear. Exercises such as removing your weight belt and replacing it will greatly increase your comfort level when these skills are called upon in more stressful situations.

Certain environmental conditions can cause stress. For example, during a dive the surf may increase in size, making a diver feel nervous when faced with an exit he feels is beyond his skill level.

By *stopping and thinking* about the situation, a fatigued and apprehensive diver can evaluate the alternate courses of actions. The solution could be as simple as dropping the weight belt, or removing the tank and pushing it in. If you stop and think in a stressful situation, you will usually see a safe way to resolve the problem.

Real or imagined dangers can cause divers stress. For example, diving in kelp without proper training. I once saw a diver freak out and bolt to the surface. I later learned that it was his first ocean dive and overheard him say, "The kelp was trying to grab me." Kelp is a plant and doesn't have a brain, so his fears were ridiculous. Learn about new environments before venturing into them.

Unfamiliar marine life can worry divers. In some parts of the world, moray eels are fairly common. In order for a moray to breathe, its mouth will be open, through which it sucks oxygen-rich water that then passes over its gills. This fact, combined with a built-in "smirk" on the eel's face, has convinced some uneducated divers that these normally docile creatures are out to get them.

Physical problems such as being out of shape, having physical injuries, or worries about family or job can cause stress.

It is important to understand the causes of stress. This is the beginning to understanding self-rescue techniques. If you realize that you are getting stressed because you are having difficulty breathing, something as simple as loosening your wetsuit can solve the problem before it worsens.

✦ THE SYMPTOMS OF STRESS

One way to recognize that you are becoming stressed is to acknowledge that you are having breathing problems. When people begin to get stressed, they hyperventilate. Hyperventilation causes carbon dioxide levels to become abnormally low; dizziness and feeling faint are common symptoms, along with a possible feeling of numbness and tingling.

Any time you feel apprehensive, you should train yourself to think consciously, "DEEP, SLOW BREATHS."

Other symptoms from stress are muscle tension and difficulties in performing simple tasks such as mask clearing. You can see symptoms of stress in others often by just looking at their eyes—a wide-eyed look is common in scared divers.

Psychological narrowing is a sign of stress. A diver may become obsessed with a single task, forgetting about other alternatives. I recently rescued a very experienced diver. When I reached him, he was frantically trying to inflate his BC, all the while screaming that he couldn't obtain buoyancy and that he was going to drown. What was happening was that his BC hose had a tear in it, so the air was escaping rather than filling his jacket. In his state of growing panic, he had become so obsessed with trying to inflate his BC that he was blind to what was happening. Complicating the situation was the fact that he had a game bag filled with lobster attached to his weight belt and was determined not to drop it. This guy was simply *not thinking!*

When gearing up prior to a dive, you may notice your buddy procrastinating or having problems with routine tasks. This could be another sign of stress due to feelings of inadequate preparation.

✦ DEALING WITH STRESS

The first and most important thing is so simple that it is often forgotten. You need to *stop* what you are doing. You don't want to make decisions in a potentially hazardous environment if you are not thinking clearly.

Often the cause of the problem will become apparent if you just stop and think. For example, the few drops of water that you weren't aware of in your mask are irritating your eyes.

Or suppose on a night dive you suddenly experience extreme vertigo (dizziness). An inexperienced diver may drop his light and rush for the surface—or where he thinks the surface is—risking embolizing or other injuries.

A much safer solution is to stop immediately what you are doing, and if possible, grab hold of something until the vertigo passes. If it doesn't, you face a few problems that may seem frightening but can be solved quickly and easily.

The next step is to think about monitoring your breathing. You may be hyperventilating, but are just unaware of it. Force yourself to take deep, *slow* breaths. It is important to get your breathing under control before you do anything.

Once your breathing is back under control, the next step is to identify what is causing your stress. Once the problem has been identified, the last step is to take action to correct it.

✦ VERTIGO

If you should experience extreme dizziness underwater, stop what you are doing and *grab hold* of something. You want to hold on to something because you may be unable to judge which way is up. Usually, the feeling of dizziness will pass in a few moments. If it doesn't, the best course of action would be to signal your buddy to assist you to the surface.

If you experience vertigo underwater, the best procedure is to hang on to something until it passes.

Entanglements such as this can be a hazard to divers.

If you are alone or if your buddy isn't available, you can tell which direction is up by following your exhaust bubbles, or watching your depth gauge and feeling for pressure changes.

A ruptured eardrum (from not equalizing properly) will cause vertigo (accompanied by severe pain while the cold water rushes in). This would be one case where pressure changes would not be felt in your ears.

Dropping your weight belt and/or inflating your BC will of course cause you to become positively buoyant.

✦ OUT OF AIR

Personally, I don't think there is *any excuse* for accidentally running out of air! Submersible pressure gauges are very reliable and usually don't fail if properly cared for. But, if it does happen, immediate and decisive action is called for. You have several choices.

Buddy Breathing involves sharing one regulator between two people. You must first alert your buddy to your situation and then let him know that you wish to buddy breathe. In my experience buddy breathing usually doesn't work. The problem is that the divers performing this skill may not have practiced it for years. I consider buddy breathing the least favorable option in an out-of-air emergency.

Of course, if you and your buddy have practiced this skill and feel confident and comfortable in its execution, then by all means use it!

Alternate Air Supplies can be carried by either you or your buddy. Alternate air supply can be in the form of additional second stages (a second stage is the part of the regulator that goes in your mouth) or completely independent units such as The Spare Air.

The procedure is to swim over to your buddy and let him know you are out of air—at which point he hands you one of his second stages. The advantage is that there's no fumbling involved passing one second stage back and forth while buddy breathing. It also eliminates one diver not having an air source while the other diver is using it. Once you have your buddy's alternate second stage, a few moments should be spent establishing a relaxed breathing pattern. When both people are calm and comfortable, a slow, controlled ascent should be made.

A Spare Air (or similar type device) is an independent mini tank and regulator that is simply handed to the diver who is out of air. Usually, these units are only good for ten breaths or so. I prefer alternate second stages.

A Free Swimming Ascent can be made if you simply swim to the surface without dropping your weight belt when you realize you are out of air. This is often the best choice if your buddy is out of reach or you're diving alone. The reason for not dropping the weight belt is that you can control your ascent, which is safer than not being able to.

Emergency Buoyant Ascents are used when the situation is more critical. The procedure here is to drop your weight belt and make a buoyant ascent to the surface. Divers in cold water will of course ascend faster (because of their full wet-suit) than divers in tropical water. When making any type of emergency ascent, it is of course very important to remember not to hold your breath.

When making emergency ascents, keep your regulator in your mouth. As surrounding water pressure decreases during your trip to the surface, you may be able to "sip" a breath or two from the tank.

ENTANGLEMENTS

Two years ago I rescued a diver who was drowning. She had become tangled up in kelp 10 feet below the surface and had spat her regulator out of her mouth. After she became unconscious, her body relaxed and untangled itself, thus allowing her to float to the surface. Fortunately, this happened near shore where rescue personnel were nearby. CPR was performed and she was completely revived without any permanent damage. The fact that her body untangled itself once she had become unconscious tells me that had she *relaxed* she could have easily untangled herself. The next question is why neither the diver in question nor her buddy was carrying a knife! When her buddy called for help he yelled, "Help! Oh God help! Please bring a knife!" The lesson is clear—always dive with a knife!

Another question is why this person spat her regulator out, since there was still air in her tank. My conclusion is that panic had caused this diver (and her buddy) to *stop thinking clearly.*

If you become entangled, stop what you are doing and

slowly remove what is restraining you. If needed, use your knife to cut yourself free.

✎ LOST BUDDY CONTACT

What would you do if while you were diving you lost contact with your buddy? You would be surprised how many divers don't discuss what they will do if this happens. A friend of mine, Jon Hardy, was recently working on shore by Catalina's Underwater Park when he was approached by a panicked man who said "Please help me! I was diving with my wife and she hasn't come up and I can't find her!"

After a few quick questions, Jon entered the water and began his search. He quickly located the man's wife, who was swimming around a wreck (while low on air), obviously looking frantically for her husband. Jon pointed to her wedding band and gave her the sign for O.K., at which point the woman immediately relaxed and they both ascended to the surface.

I recommend that you and your buddy agree that if you lose contact with each other, you will search for one minute and then surface. This helps to avoid unneeded anxiety and worry.

✎ SURFACE RESCUES

This involves assisting a diver who is on the surface and in trouble or on his way to being in trouble. As you approach the diver, stop about 10 feet in front of him and ask him, "How are you doing?" The reply will often dictate what you do next. For instance, a response of, "I'm tired and I don't think I can make it back to the boat" would indicate that all you need to do is tow him back. Whereas a wide-eyed, panicked diver, frantically slashing at the surrounding kelp with his knife screaming, "I'm all tangled up!" would call for a rather different response.

Often, you can assist divers on the surface by simply telling them what to do. Commands such as: "Drop your weight belt" or "Put the regulator back in your mouth and I'll tow you back to the boat" will resolve the situation.

If the situation merits it, you can approach the diver and physically assist him. On quite a few occasions, I've approached divers who were in so much self-induced trouble that immediate action was necessary to prevent them from drowning. The first course of action is to establish positive buoyancy. Undo the weight belt, pull it clear of the body and let it go. It's usually best not to tell him you are doing this since he will probably argue that he doesn't want to lose a $30 weight belt.

Once the weight belt is removed, the next step is to inflate the BC. You would be surprised. These acts can be performed in seconds.

After buoyancy has been established, figure out what else may be causing the discomfort and try to resolve the problem.

✦ UNCONSCIOUS DIVER

If you approach a diver on the surface and he is floating face down and does not appear to be moving, start to yell and splash at him as you get close. It may be that the person is all right and just preoccupied.

If you don't get a response as soon as you reach the diver, immediately turn him over, drop his weight belt, inflate the BC if needed, and remove his mask and regulator. As you are doing this, you also want to remove any of your own gear that may hinder you in performing the rescue. For instance, I would immediately drop my weight belt and remove my tank to jettison as much weight and drag as possible.

The first and most important priority is to begin mouth to mouth resuscitation. While it's not possible to give CPR chest compressions while in the water, it is possible to give mouth to mouth resuscitation.

The procedure is to lace your left arm through the victim's left arm (from the front) and to place your hand on the back of his head for support. Your other hand is used to seal his nose and tilt his head back, which will open the airway. This procedure also works using the opposite side of the body (with your right arm).

NOTE: It is almost impossible to learn CPR solely from a book. Hands-on experience is needed. For more information on CPR, contact your local Red Cross and enroll in one of their courses.

Once you have started mouth to mouth resuscitation, you should transport the victim back to the boat or shore immediately.

If you should encounter an unconscious diver underwater, the first priority is to get him to the surface. Absence of exhaust bubbles is an immediate indication that the person is not breathing. Grab him from behind, pull his weight belt free (and yours if need be), and "ride" him to the surface. It is important to place one hand under his chin and tilt his head back. This keeps his airway open and allows expanding air to escape. Once on the surface the procedure is the same as previously noted for an unconscious diver.

When you get back to the boat, getting the person out of the water (if you are alone) can be tricky. The best procedure is to cross his wrists so you can hold them in one hand while climbing out of the water yourself. Then hold his wrists while the person faces away from you and lift him out of the water.

⌒ DROWNING

Symptoms of a drowning include a lot of white foam coming out of the nose and mouth. If the froth is bloody, then the possibility the person has also embolized should be considered. Upon reaching the victim in the water, clear his airway and begin mouth to mouth resuscitation. You will need to roll the person onto one side to allow water to drain from the chest; doing this while still in the water is difficult at best, but you should begin mouth to mouth in the water as soon as you reach the victim. The foam you'll see is the water coming up, and more liquid will most likely come out when you begin respirations.

Once on shore (or on the boat), full CPR should begin, emergency personnel should be notified, and immediate arrangements for transportation to a medical facility should be made.

⌒ CUTS AND SEVERE BLEEDING

Coral, jagged rocks, rusty shipwrecks, broken glass, and bites from marine life can all cause severe cuts. If the cut is deep enough, severe bleeding may result.

It is important to *stop the bleeding* immediately! Direct pressure should be applied to the wound. Ideally, medical gauze should be used, but in an emergency a shirt or any other garment will serve as a makeshift compress. If nothing is available use your hands. If clothing or gauze material is being used and blood begins to clot on the compress, do not remove it. Leave it in place while the victim is transported to a medical facility.

It may be helpful to elevate the part of the body that has been cut. Raise the limb above the victim's heart, using gravity to help reduce the blood pressure and loss of blood.

Pressure on a main artery above the cut can also be used to retard bleeding. A tourniquet should not be applied unless loss of life is imminent!

If foreign matter such as bits of coral or glass can be seen in the wound, they should be removed. Do not however, attempt to remove any foreign material that is deeply embedded. This should be done only by qualified medical personnel.

➤ SHOCK

Water-related and blood-loss injuries may cause the victim to go into traumatic shock. Shock is recognizable in the early stages by changes in the color of the nail beds and skin. The skin may also be moist and clammy and the victim's pulse will usually be high and faint. Other symptoms include irregular breathing, weakness, and vomiting.

Maintain body temperature and administer fluids unless the victim is unconscious or has been vomiting; oxygen should also be supplied.

If a head injury has been sustained, do not allow the victim's head to lie lower than his heart. Often the type of injury will dictate body position, but when in doubt have the person lie on his back with the head and shoulders raised.

➤ DECOMPRESSION SICKNESS

Symptoms of the bends usually begin shortly after a dive, but may not show up for over forty-eight hours. Symptoms include: localized pain (often in the joints), skin rashes, respiratory difficulties, numbness, speech impairment, and shock.

Treat the victim for shock and administer 100% oxygen. Do not attempt to "recompress" the victim in the water. If complications were to arise while submerged (such as heart attack or stroke), they would be impossible to treat.

As soon as decompression sickness is suspected, arrangements for transportation to a recompression chamber should begin immediately.

✦ HYPOTHERMIA

Hypothermia is a potential hazard for divers who may be submerged for extended periods of time in the water. Early symptoms are shivering, goosebumps, and simply feeling cold. Shiver occurs because your body is trying to create heat, so the muscles "rub" together and the friction generates heat.

If you don't get out of the water at this point, the body's blood starts to withdraw to the vital organs (vasoconstriction). Extremities, such as hands and feet, become white from lack of blood.

Treatment involves getting the victim out of the water, removing wet clothes and drying them, and putting the person near a heat source. The use of hot water bottles and other extreme sources of heat should be avoided.

Give liquids, but not alcohol; alcohol is a vasoconstrictor and should not be administered.

✦ HYPERTHERMIA

Prolonged exposure to the sun may lead to heat exhaustion, also known as sunstroke. Victims of sunstroke will usually feel dizzy and have red skin—you may actually feel the heat coming off them. The skin is red because blood is coming near the surface in an attempt to cool the body off. Sunstroke victims should be cooled off; get them in the shade and administer liquids.

If you travel to the tropics, or are planning to spend a day in the sun (such as on a boat), make sure you take the proper precautions to avoid heat stroke. Wearing a hat and drinking lots of water are two good deterrents.

✦ EMBOLISMS

To competently treat a full-blown lung over-expansion injury in the field is difficult at best. However, if you find yourself faced with a embolism victim, begin CPR if necessary,

If a serious injury occurs far from shore, a helicopter evacuation may be called for.

Divers climb back on board The Charisma *after a dive.*

administer oxygen, treat for shock, alert rescue personnel, and arrange for immediate transportation to medical facilities.

⌁ HELICOPTER EVACUATION

If you are on a boat and not near shore and someone is seriously injured, he will probably be evacuated by helicopter. This is usually done by the Coast Guard, police, or military personnel.

To prepare for a helicopter evacuation, remove any non-essential antennas, and anything else that might interfere with the lowering of the basket/stretcher. Also, secure any loose gear on deck. The idea is not to have anything lying around that could be blown loose by the down wash from the helicopter rotor.

Allow the stretcher to touch the deck of the ship before anyone handles it. This allows it to "ground," which prevents handlers from receiving an electrical shock.

⌁ LEG CRAMPS

A leg cramp is not a critical emergency, but can be highly annoying. To relieve a leg cramp while diving, grab the end of your fin and straighten your leg. Usually, the cramp will be relieved within a few moments.

⌁ SEASICKNESS

While not a medical emergency, being seasick can ruin an otherwise enjoyable day of diving. What happens when you get seasick is that the motion of the boat causes the fluid in the semicircular canals of your inner ear to move around. Since this is abnormal, your brain thinks something is wrong. So, it wants to purge the contents of your stomach and you feel nauseated.

Seasick pills semi-solidify the fluid in your inner ear, thus preventing the above scenario. Some seasick pills will make you drowsy, so I recommend you try them before you go out on the boat. Also, people with pulmonary illnesses should consult a physician before taking any seasick medication.

If you get seasick try to stay in the fresh air and watch the horizon.

CHAPTER 9

Dive Specialties

So now you're certified and you're wondering what types of diving to try next! Most people find that after they've done a few dives they need to get involved in some type of underwater specialty to maintain interest. Don't misunderstand, you could spend a lifetime sightseeing and still not see everything the oceans have to offer. But if you're looking for some other possibilities, how about...

➤ *BOAT DIVING*

Boat diving gives you the means to visit places that would otherwise be inaccessible. Vanuatu, for example, is made up of a chain of islands 500 miles west of Fiji. Since most of the islands are underdeveloped and don't have hotels, airports, or any modern facilities, a support vessel capable of open ocean crossings is needed to dive these islands.

Diving off a large support vessel in exotic locations (such as Vanuatu) will give you the opportunity to dive sites that have *never* been visited by humans before!

Dive boats range from 10-foot kayaks that can be launched from shore to large oceanic cruise ships. Basically, the bigger the boat, the more comfortable you'll be during your trip.

Live-aboards are sort of the ultimate dive boats; *The Coriolis* (see picture) is a good example. They're called live-aboards because you actually live on the ship for a week or two. The advantage to this is that you can cover hundreds of miles and see a wide variety of dive sights. Usually the ship is moved at night while you sleep.

Diving off a ship this size is usually done from Zodiacs, which are available around the clock to take divers to nearby sites. One reason for this is that the "mother ship" destroys anything it anchors on (due to its anchor size). Also, much of the diving is done from a live boat. Divers are dropped off and dive with the current. The "live boat" then follows the diver's bubbles and picks them up at the end of the dive. Obviously, live boat diving would be impractical and dangerous from a boat as large as *The Coriolis*.

Food on live-aboard boats is usually excellent. The usual routine is a breakfast of choice, served from 6:00 to 9:00 A.M., followed by the morning's dives. Lunch is waiting when divers return in the afternoon. Dinner may consist of local fresh catch and an international selection of familiar dishes. Meals are commonly included in the price of diving from a live-aboard. (If they're not, they should be.) Most boats have a round-the-clock bar and the usual procedure is to settle your bill at the end of the charter.

Sleeping accommodations range from deluxe cabins with queen-sized double beds and private baths to the less expensive multiple occupancy bunk rooms. The less expensive rooms usually share a common toilet and shower, but a sink may be in the room.

Some things that should be included in any live-aboard package are: 1. Tanks and weights. Obviously transporting your tank and weight belt when traveling overseas would be inconvenient. 2. Unlimited air fills: the boat shouldn't nickel and dime you every time you need a tank filled. 3. All meals. You will probably have to pay for snacks and additional beverages, but no live-aboard should charge you by the individual meal. 4. Transportation from the airport to the boat and back. This is common practice for most dive resorts. This is all basic stuff; any live-aboard that tries to charge you individually for the above items should probably be avoided.

⤙ DAY BOATS

California, Florida, and Hawaii all have year-round diving available. Because they have such a large population of divers, each state also has a large fleet of dive boats. These day boats range from 20-foot "six-packs" (carrying up to six passengers) to 85-foot vessels capable of carrying about forty divers.

Passage on day boats can be booked through local dive shops or directly through the boats themselves. *Dive Boat Calendar* is an excellent source of information on boat itineraries and how to book passage; it is sold at most dive shops.

Catalina Island is 26 miles off the coast of southern California. San Nicolas Island lies 66 miles off the mainland. A boat leaving the mainland for Catalina would depart around 7:00 A.M. while a boat whose destination was San Nicolas

There are a vast number of locations around the world that divers can explore.

would depart at 1:00 A.M. Boat departure times depend on destination, so be sure to ask when you can board and when the boat leaves. You may be able to board at 8:00 P.M. and go to sleep, even if the boat is leaving at 1:00 A.M. the next morning.

Unlike resort live-aboard boats, day boats usually do not supply tanks and weights...nor do they rent them. When diving from "open" (anybody can sign up) boats, you need to be self-sufficient, have all your own gear prior to boarding, and be capable of handling the types of conditions found where the boat is going.

The usual routine is to sign in upon boarding. This sheet will be used for roll calls before the boat leaves a dive site. There will probably be a number where you sign your name. For the duration of the trip you may be referred to by your number when you buy air or food. You should write your name and number on a piece of tape (that's usually supplied) and stick it on your tank. This enables the person filling the tanks to keep track of how many air fills you have so you can be charged for them at the end of the day. Air fills are often not included in the cost of day boats.

There may also be a bunk sign-in sheet. This enables you to designate one of the bunk beds below deck as yours. If there is no bunk sign-in sheet, putting an article of clothing on a bed claims it as yours. Wet dive gear is not allowed below decks. Your dive bag should be stowed wherever the dive master designates.

Most of the larger boats have a galley and food is available around the clock. When ordering, you'll most likely give your number. At the end of the day your food and air fill costs will be tallied.

When diving from an anchored boat, the safest thing to do is to descend down the anchor line. This not only gives you a point of reference, but also prevents you from drifting during your descent. It's a good idea to work your dive out from the anchor and return to the anchor at the end of your dive. This is easier than you'd imagine. Obviously a compass is a useful tool, but there are also natural navigation aids, such as ripples in the sand, slope of the bottom, and direction of current.

Returning to and ascending up the anchor line will avoid a long and tiring surface swim and give you a reference point during your ascent. I recommend a five minute safety stop at 15 feet on all dives. Hanging onto the anchor line allows you to hold your position accurately rather than drifting aimlessly in open water.

Entering the Water

The dive master will tell you the preferred method of entering the water. But basically, keep this in mind: look for the safest and easiest way in and use it. If diving from a small boat (such as a Zodiac), you may do a back roll. The important things to remember here are to keep your chin on your chest (so you don't bang your head on the tank), keep your hands on your mask (so you don't lose it), and put all gauges and loose hoses over the side of the boat before you roll in. I once saw a diver roll into the water only to be hung up by his gauge console that had remained hooked on a rope. The poor guy was hanging upside down, head underwater, feet sticking up in the air, and probably would have drowned if we hadn't unhooked him!

When entering off a larger boat, you'll probably do a giant stride. To do a giant stride you simply step off the boat in an upright position, hitting the water feet first. The idea is to hit the water with your legs apart (as if walking) and to bring them together on impact to stop your descent.

On all entries, it's important to inflate your BC so you'll be buoyant when you hit the water.

Six-packs are a great way to go diving for a day because the group is small enough that you can build a custom day around your needs as a group. My friends and I often charter a small six-pack to go chase down dolphins so we can get in the water and photograph them.

WRECK DIVING

When people think about scuba diving, probably one of the first images that comes to mind is that of a sunken shipwreck laden with treasures, patrolled by hungry man-eating sharks! Wreck diving captures the public's imagination. It's also one of the most enjoyable underwater activities available to certified divers.

Wreck diving can be divided into three categories. Non-penetration refers to dives where the ship is not entered and is recommended to all divers who do not have the specialized training required for any overhead environment.

A dive where you enter the wreck but keep the entry point within sight at all times is referred to as light penetration. I don't recommend you enter a wreck at all without proper training. One of the main problems encountered is silt. Silt stirred up from a diver's fins can quickly and unexpectedly cloud up a room so that the entry point can no longer be seen. A diver's exhaust bubbles can also stir up silt.

Deep penetration is a term used to describe dives that extend deep into a wreck, well beyond the entry point. Safety lines are an absolute must. If a diver becomes disoriented, following his safety line out will be his only means of escape. Light is entirely supplied by whatever flashlights the diver carries. Redundancy is a wreck diver's (and cave diver's) favorite word. Imagine being deep inside a wreck only to have your flashlight go out. Obviously, wreck divers need to carry back-up lights!

The use of a secondary air supply (such as an AIR II) is recommended for all diving activities but is critical for wreck divers. If you run out of air inside a wreck, you will not be able to ascend directly to the surface, and if you don't have a secondary air supply. . .you're going to have a problem.

➤ CAVE DIVING

All the rules that apply to wreck diving apply to cave diving. Probably, experienced divers have accidentally lost their lives by wandering into a cave without thinking about possible consequences. The result is often death if they don't have adequate training and gear. Do not under any circumstances enter a cave without first obtaining competent instruction from a certified cave diving instructor.

If you dive a cave (or any overhead environment) and find an air space trapped in the ceiling, resist the temptation to take the regulator out of your mouth and breathe. The air may be bad, or even toxic. Some places, such as Palau, have caves that dive guides regularly take divers to and are obviously okay to visit.

➤ ICE DIVING

If you're a hardy soul and looking for something adventurous. . .or live in Minnesota, then ice diving may be for you.

All the rules about redundancy in overhead environments apply here. Ice diving should also, under no circumstances, be attempted without first obtaining quality instruction from a certified ice diving instructor.

A dry suit is mandatory to provide adequate protection against the cold water. If you have never been diving in a dry suit, it would be an excellent idea to first do a few dives in warmer water to learn the mechanics and slightly different techniques used with this type of equipment. For example, when your feet are higher than your head, the air in a dry suit rushes to your feet and can prevent you from returning to an upright position. The solution is to tuck into a ball and roll into an upright position.

Ice diving is usually done on a lake and first requires cutting a large hole that divers will enter and exit from. Usually, a large tent is set up over the hole once it's been cut to provide some protection from the elements. Obviously, safety lines are a critical part of ice diving.

It's also important to have safety divers standing by to assist in the event that a diver becomes separated from his safety line. If this happens, the person in the water should hold his position under the ice, at the surface where the lost diver's air supply will last longer. Searching for the exit hole

Some divers may choose to spend their time underwater hunting for lobster.

will often result in swimming farther away, making rescue unlikely.

The usual procedure is for safety divers, attached to a line, to enter the water and swim in a circle. After each completed circle, a tender on the surface lets out another 10 feet of line. This increases the diameter of the circle in which the safety diver is swimming. The idea is that with each consecutive circle, the safety diver covers new territory without becoming disoriented and will eventually come upon the lost diver.

Visibility under an ice pack is often tremendous, which is one of the attractions of ice diving.

✦ GAME COLLECTING

The ocean is filled with things to eat. Hunting is one of the activities that many divers take up after they've logged a few dives past their basic certification course.

It's important to check what your local fish and game regulations are for the species you intend to hunt. At a minimum, you'll need to obtain a fishing license, which can be bought at most sporting goods stores.

Lobster Hunting

Lobster hunting (because lobsters look like large bugs, divers refer to it as bug hunting) requires a pair of gloves and a game bag. The best time to catch lobster is at night, so you'll also need a good underwater flashlight. Lobster can usually be found in rocky areas. They spend their days hiding in the rocks and come out in the open at night to hunt for food. It's during their nightly outings that they are easiest to catch.

What you do is swim along the bottom until you see a "bug." Have your buddy shine his light directly in front of the lobster; this usually causes them to freeze momentarily, allowing you the opportunity to grab him swiftly. Gloves are needed because the lobster's tail is sharp enough to pinch and cut your skin as it frantically flexes it trying to swim away. Depending on where you're diving, the bugs may also have claws; if they do, beware! Lobsters swim backwards so it's important to place them in the bag backwards. One of my best laughs underwater came when a buddy of mine put a lobster in his game bag front claws first. When he let it go, the enraged bug immediately swam out of the bag at full velocity, hitting him squarely in the face!

The best procedure is to place the lobster in the bag, then have your buddy hold the bug from outside, while you remove your hand and close the bag.

Abalone

Abalone are one of the easiest creatures to capture. The hard part is learning to see them since they blend in well with their surroundings.

You'll need an "Ab" iron to pry the abalone free from the rocks. Abalone are hemophiliacs and they will bleed to death if cut. An Ab iron is designed not to cut the animal so you can replant it on its rock if it measures under size.

Since abalone come in a variety of species (in California there are five, for example), each with different size and quantity limits, be sure to check with local fish and game officials for a list of current regulations.

Scallops

Scallops are another often collected shellfish and they're easy to catch because they don't swim. Since the inside of the scallop's shell is orange, the best way to find scallops is to swim along, keeping an eye out for the orange color. When you approach them they will often close their shells, their movement giving another indication of where they are. Once you have established that the scallop meets with local fish and game regulations, you'll need a small pick to break the scallop free of the reef.

Flat Fish

Halibut, rock, sole, turbot, and flounder are all members of the family *Bothidae,* which is made up of various species of flat fish. These animals can be found almost anywhere there is a sandy bottom. Novice divers often swim right over large flat fish since they blend in with their environment so well.

To catch one, swim along about 3 feet off the bottom and look for an outline of the fish. Flat fish often cover themselves up with sand, leaving only their eyes exposed. If you swim too close to the bottom, you may not have enough perspective to see the fish. Once you have spotted your prey—

When taking pictures of large marine life such as this sleeping angel shark, shown here being lifted by Jon Hardy, it's useful to "pre-set" your focus. The Nikonos is ideal for this.

A diver displays a large scallop

and have measured it to establish that it meets fish and game regulations—the best way to catch it is to spear it from above, thus pinning the fish to the sand. The next step is to reach under the animal, grab your spear, and put the fish in a game bag or fish stringer.

A fish stringer is a metal loop that hooks onto your weight belt and enables you to hook fish by running the loop through their mouth and out one of their gills. I don't recommend this practice (especially with large fish) because the fish occasionally tear loose. Game bags are usually made of some kind of mesh material and come in a variety of sizes. The bag can be hooked to your weight belt, or a dive buddy can carry it.

It is not a good idea to stay in the water for prolonged periods of time with a bloody, struggling fish strung on your belt. In the unlikely event there is a shark nearby, the scent and fish movement could attract them. The best plan of action is to return speared fish to the boat as soon as possible. If a shark does show up and become a pest, give him the fish and get out of the water.

There are numerous species of fish that are hunted by spear fishermen. What you hunt depends largely on what part of the world you dive in. The techniques, however, remain the same. When stalking potential prey, approach from underneath, taking advantage of the fish's blind spot. Many spear fisherman hunt exclusively while skin diving (no scuba tank), claiming the exhaust bubbles from tanks scare large fish away.

The type of gun you use depends on the type of environment you are in and the size of the fish you hunt. Small to mid-size species are often found along coastal reefs and in the kelp beds of temperate seas, while larger species are usually hunted in open water. Pole spears and small to mid-size guns are used in shore, while the larger, multiple-banded guns are used to hunt the larger species in open water.

NIGHT DIVING

Entering the ocean at three in the morning armed with only a flashlight and a sense of adventure is an exhilarating experience! A diver's first night dive is usually one of the more memorable moments in his diving career.

The two important considerations when diving at night

are: 1. being able to see while underwater and, 2. being able to see your entry/exit point while in the water. One of the first times I did a night dive off the beach, my buddy and I were unable to identify where our car was from offshore. Looking back at a pitch-black beach, it was impossible to identify any landmarks that we took for granted during the day. When we reached shore, we were unsure whether our car was north or south of us. As a result we had to do a lot of walking with tanks and weights in the middle of the night.

To avoid experiencing a similar scenario, be sure to mark your exit point with a light that can easily be seen from offshore. Car headlights can be turned on by an onshore buddy after a pre-determined amount of time, flashlights or strobes can be placed on shore where they can be seen by divers in the water. I use two Cyalume™ Chem-lights. These chemical lights come in plastic tubes that glow when you break and shake them. They come in various colors with red, green, and blue being the most common colors used by divers. I put red and green Chem-lights about 40 feet apart on shore. This gives me a clear exit point at the end of my dive.

When night diving from a boat, the boat should be well lit so divers will have no trouble spotting it quickly from the water.

The Chem-lights should also be attached to divers in the water. Taping one to your snorkel allows you to be spotted from shore or from a boat if your primary light should fail. Attaching one to your tank valve helps your dive buddy locate you when you have your back to him and he can't see your flashlight. Obviously, Chem-lights are useful to divers and I recommend you carry a few in your dive bag.

My favorite dive light is Darrel Allan's Bug Diver™. It's powered by ten D cell batteries and is one of the most rugged and powerful lights made. There is a wide variety of underwater flashlights on the market. I do a lot of diving in cold, turbid water, which is why I prefer powerful lights. If you're diving in warm water with 100-foot plus visibility, a small low-power light may be adequate.

Some lights (such as the Bug Diver™) come in either metal or plastic. Generally the metal lights are negatively buoyant (they sink if you drop them) and the plastic lights are positive (they float). There are advantages and disadvantages to both. Some people like a light that floats because it's easy to find floating on the surface if they drop it during the dive. Be-

This fire coral can deliver a painful sting and is common in many tropical seas.

Two blue sharks mirror each other.

cause I tether my light to my wrist, I like negatively buoyant lights that don't float up into my face if I want to let them go. Bagging a struggling lobster is hard enough without being blinded by your own light!

If you want to explain something to your buddy while night diving, remember to shine your light on yourself when you give him hand signals. Many people point their flashlights at their buddy and then proceed to signal; the problem here is that by shining the light in your buddy's face, you blind him, making it impossible for him to see what it is you're trying to communicate.

Carrying a smaller secondary back-up light is a good idea. I carry a small flashlight strapped to my forearm. Usually, I don't need to use it, but on the few occasions when my primary light has failed, it has proved useful.

BEACH DIVING

Technically, beach diving could be defined as any dive that takes place from shore, but what I am referring to are dives done from shore where there are waves. The main considerations are how big the waves are and in what sequence they're hitting shore. By observing the surf line, a recognizable pattern may be observed. For example, four large waves may be followed by two small waves. This pattern may keep repeating itself. Obviously, it would be better to time your entry so that you go out when the small waves are rolling in. There may also be a lull (a period of no surf) after every few waves. This would be another good time to make your entry.

The surf line is one place where there is little time to stop and evaluate your situation. Basically, if you get munched by a wave, your only options are to kick out past the breaking surf or to kick, crawl, and claw your way back to shore. Remember to keep your regulator in your mouth and your mask on. This way if you do get pushed down by a large breaker, you'll be able to see and breathe. It will help to keep one hand on your mask as the waves hit you. This will prevent your mask from being pulled off your head by the force of the water!

CHAPTER 10

Cooking What You Catch

It's surprising how many divers don't know how to cook what they catch. They bring up a couple of pounds of fish, lobster, and other game and—after having their picture taken with their catch—take it home with the intention of "giving it to a friend."

I've been given fish on a couple of occasions after wandering into a dive shop where I wasn't known. Usually the fish-giver explains, "I speared this halibut off the beach but I don't eat fish and would you like it?" While this approach is better than the guy who just leaves the fish for dead after the sport of catching it, why not learn how to cook what you catch? And remember, don't take anything you can't eat yourself!

Some divers let seafood go to waste purely because they don't know how to clean or cook it. I've gotten calls from friends explaining that they've caught a bunch of lobster and want to know how to cook them.

While this chapter can't cover every method and recipe for preparing seafood, it should give you a couple of ideas on where to begin. In addition to what follows there are some excellent cookbooks available that deal exclusively with seafood recipes.

ABALONE

Abalone are highly sought after by divers in various parts of the world. Cleaning a freshly-caught abalone is relatively simple. To remove the animal from its shell use a wooden spoon or an "ab iron" to pry it free. Some people claim that first putting the animal in fresh water anesthetizes it as it dies, making the task of removal easier.

The next step is to trim off all the guts and the darker colored "foot" the animal uses to attach itself to rocks. Basically, cut off everything except the light colored meat that makes up the center of the abalone. Now slice the meat into round steaks about ¼-inch thick.

An abalone is basically one big muscle. If you don't pound the steaks to tenderize them your jaw is going to get a workout! A wooden mallet works well, but if you're on a boat the butt of your dive knife or ab iron will also get the job done. Simply pound each of the steaks on both sides a couple of times.

Now you are ready to begin!

Galley Ab Special

The first time most divers taste fresh abalone, this is the way it's cooked—often in the galley of a dive boat.

Cut the steaks previously prepared into ¼ inch-long strips. Melt half a stick of butter in a frying pan and then add the abalone strips. Sauté on each side for about thirty seconds and remove. Put the strips on a paper towel to remove some of the grease. If you have it, a little garlic powder in the butter is a good idea.

Seasick Special

I imagine the rather unappetizing name of this recipe comes from the fact that dive boats used to use soda crackers (which were always on hand for seasick victims) instead of bread crumbs.

You'll need to beat an egg or two together and have some flour and bread crumbs.

Dip the abalone first in the flour, then in the egg, and then in the bread crumbs. The idea is to completely coat the steak in the bread crumbs.

Now fry the steaks in oil or butter for about twenty-five seconds on each side.

Serve with a salad and some white wine and you're an instant gourmet!

Val's Abalone Cordon Bleu

This was first shown to me by my brother Val and I'm still surprised at how well it came out. You will need two slices of ham and a slice of mozzarella cheese for each serving, along with two eggs, milk, and some flour.

Preheat your oven to 400°F.

Beat the eggs in a bowl and then add a splash of milk.

Sandwich two slices of ham with a slice of cheese between two abalone steaks and then dip the whole thing in the egg, and then in the butter.

Now fry in oil on each side until lightly brown. Add whatever seasoning you like while frying. After your "sandwich" is brown, place it in the preheated oven for eight minutes.

LOBSTER

Contrary to popular belief, lobsters don't feel pain when they're boiled; they don't have pain-sensitive nerves. If, however, you want to kill a lobster before boiling, place it in a pot of fresh warm water. The lobster essentially goes to sleep and dies.

Another way to kill a lobster is to push a knife quickly between its eyes, which kills it instantly.

Boiled Lobster

This is the easiest way to cook a lobster and can be done on a beach, a boat, or just about anywhere. All you need is a fire, a pot of water, and some lobsters!

Put enough fresh water in a pot to cover the lobster—or lobsters—completely and bring it to a boil.

Now put the lobsters in the boiling water; figure on about six to seven minutes cooking time per pound of lobster.

Remove the lobsters from the water, crack open the shell, dip the meat in some melted butter, and eat! A great way to end a night of diving off the beach.

Grilled Lobster

To do this you need to first cut the lobster in half and separate the tail from the rest of the body.

Place the lobster tails on the grill, meat side down. Cook until the meat feels firm.

Michel's Lobster Soup

This is a quick and easy way to cook lobster. You will need: About four pounds of lobster meat, milk, and heavy whipping cream.

Cut the lobster meat into ½-inch squares. Now melt a little butter in a frying pan and sauté the lobster meat until it turns red (usually three to four minutes).

Combine six cups of milk and two cups of the cream in a large pot and heat it up (but don't boil).

When the liquid is hot, add the lobster meat and whatever spices you like!

⌒ CLEANING FISH

Cleaning a fish is a quick and easy operation once you get the hang of it. The quickest way to learn is to watch someone do it once or twice. If, however, you can't find an experienced fish dresser to help, then go get a thin, sharp knife and read on! Lay the fish on its side and make a cut starting just in front of the tail and continuing along its belly to just behind the head. The trick is not to cut too deeply to avoid bursting the animal's intestines and spoiling the taste of the meat.

Now reach inside the fish and pull out all the guts. They should come out easily; occasionally you may need to make a few cuts to remove the kidney that lies along the animal's backbone. Rinse out the cavity with fresh water.

The gills are the slits behind the head. If you want to leave the head on the fish you should cut out the orange gills. Do this by making a cut below the gill slits and working your way up until the gills are cut free.

Once the guts have been removed the fish is said to be field dressed. You can stop at this point if you want to cook the fish whole.

If you want to make fillets there are two ways to go. The

first and quickest is to start at the tail and remove one side of the fish in one cut by dragging the knife between the bone in the animal's center and the flesh. Don't cut through the head, but cut up and out before you reach it. You then turn the fish over and repeat the cut.

The one drawback is that a lot of meat is left on the bones — thus wasted. Another method is to remove the fillet slowly. . . working with your knife as you go. The idea is to stay as close to the bones as possible. Usually the head is cut off before filleting. This method is used by restaurants that dress out large fish and want the least amount of waste.

If the fish is big enough you can now slice the fillet into steaks.

Cleaning a flat fish such as a halibut is a little different. Turn the fish light side up so that the eyes are facing you. Now make a cut at the top of the fish behind the head. Continue to work the fillet free, cutting between the bone and the flesh. When you've removed the fillet, turn the fish over and repeat the process.

You don't need to gut the fish unless you want to cook it whole. To gut a flat fish first cut the head off. Then, starting forward of the tail, apply downward pressure and slide your hand forward along the bottom of the fish. The guts will come out the front of the fish. Pull them clear and rinse the cavity with fresh water.

To skin the fillets, lat them skin down and make a cut between the skin and meat at the tail end of the fillet. Now gently pull the skin free, cutting with the knife as you go.

ROCKFISH

There is a variety of species of rockfish that can be eaten. All of them can be cooked in a similar fashion.

Steamed Rockfish

You can do this with either fillets or an entire fish (gutted of course). Lightly coat the fillets with oil and then sprinkle garlic and chopped scallions on them. If you're working with a whole fish, you can also stuff the scallions and garlic inside the fish.

Boil four cups of water in a wok, and then put the fish on a steamer rack on top and cover. Cook about twenty minutes.

Rocky's Rockfish

Rocky's Rockfish was shown to me by the owner of Scuba-haus during his Fourth of July barbecue.

Melt a quarter stick of butter in a large frying pan and then add some chopped up shallots. After about a minute add half a glass of white wine. Cook until the liquid begins to reduce and then add a dash of crushed tarragon. Drain the liquid and set it aside to be used as a sauce. Lightly coat the rockfish fillets with oil and grill for about five minutes. When done pour the sauce on top and serve!

Rockfish Salad

Fill a frying pan about ½ inch deep with water and boil, adding a dash of garlic. When the water is boiling add the rockfish fillets and cook for about four minutes.

Once done, remove the fillets from the water and let cool. Cut into chunks and toss into a salad.

FISH FILLETS

What follows are some ways of cooking fish fillets that will work regardless of the species of fish being used. Naturally some recipes will taste better with certain types of fish and this is shown in the recipe's title when appropriate.

The Greenfield Special

For this recipe you will need: three large potatoes, peeled and thinly sliced; three onions, sliced; and two cups of whipping cream.

Preheat your oven to 400°F. and cover a baking dish with a layer of butter.

Now put a layer of sliced potatoes on the bottom of the dish and then add a layer of onions on top. Put the fish fillets on top of the onions. Now add another layer of sliced onions, and then potatoes again. Pour the cream on top and bake for twenty-five minutes.

After twenty-five minutes reduce the oven tenperature to 325°F. and bake for another eighty minutes (until the potatoes are brown).

Cary's Sheephead Sunrise

Sheephead is a common fish in California...and in my opinion, it is definitely an acquired taste. However, my friend Cory insists it is delicious when prepared this way and claims he likes to eat it for breakfast before a dive!

Mix a ¼ to ½ cup (depending on how many fillets you have) of olive oil with a dash of lemon juice and some ground up oregano and black pepper.

Put the mixture in a shallow dish and add your fillets. Let them sit in liquid for thirty minutes and then turn them over and let them sit for an hour.

Now fry the fillets in a pan lightly coated with oil.

Grilled Fish Fillets

This will work with just about anything. Lightly cover the fillets with melted butter and sprinkle some parsley on each side.

Place on the grill and turn over every two minutes. When the fillets become flaky when tested with a fork they are done!

Fried Garlic Fish

As the name implies, this one's for garlic lovers.

Put a thin layer of olive oil in a frying pan and heat it up. Add three cloves of thinly sliced garlic and sauté until the garlic softens.

Squirt lemon on each side of the fish fillets and fry on each side until done.

Grilled Fish Fillets with Nuts and Cheese

For this one you will need: Some cashews, about a pound of blue cheese, a cup of cream cheese, and about a cup of farmer cheese.

First fry the cashews in a pan until they go brown on both sides. When they're done, remove the nuts and smash them into smaller chunks.

Mix the nuts and various cheeses together and then coat the fish fillets with this paste. Lay some slices of lemon on the grill and then place the fillets on top of them. (Orange slices will work as well.) Cook for about six minutes.

The Trauer's Cod and Tomatoes Special

Put a layer of olive oil in a frying pan and heat it up. Now add ½ cup of water, seven pearl onions, some rosemary, salt and pepper, and ½ cup of white wine. Lightly coat the cod fillets with flour and then put them in the pan and cook for about four minutes.

Now add a can of stewed tomatoes and cook for an additional five minutes.

HALIBUT

Since halibut spend much of their time lying motionless on the bottom, they are easily caught by observant spearfishermen. The fact they also taste terrific make them one of the more popular game fish. Many of the recipes that follow will work with other species of flat fish.

Heidi's Halibut Special

You'll need to keep the bones from the fish to make the "fish stock" needed for this one.

In a large pot melt a quarter stick of butter and then sauté one chopped onion, two carrots, and some chopped celery. When done, add twelve cups of water.

Stir in eleven peppercorns, a bay leaf, and the fish bones. Let the stock simmer for twenty minutes and then strain the vegetables and bones out.

Keep the stock simmering and add the halibut steaks. Cook for about five minutes.

While the halibut is cooking melt ½ stick of butter in a frying pan and add a crushed clove of garlic and a dash of lemon juice.

When the halibut is cooked, remove it from the stock and serve it with the butter/garlic poured on top.

Pierre's Grilled Halibut with Pasta

Fry some walnuts until brown. When they're done, crush them and set aside. Melt some butter and squeeze some lime juice into it.

Paint the halibut with the butter and lime juice and grill. While the fish is on the grill, cook the pasta noodles.

Serve the halibut with the crushed walnuts sprinkled on top and the pasta on the side.

⌁ CRAB

There are numerous species of crab that can be eaten. What you catch depends largely on what part of the country you live in. Regardless of what species you're dealing with, the cooking procedure remains the same. Usually, you'll cook the crab whole and then prepare it in some manner. Here are some of the more popular recipes.

Bernard's Boiled Crab

It's as easy as boiling a pot of water and dropping the crab in. When it floats to the surface, it's done.

Pull the legs off the cooked crab, crack the shell, and pull the meat out. Serve with melted butter.

Chipper's Crab Cake Surprise

To make these crab burgers you will need: one egg, ¾ cup of bread crumbs, two chopped up scallions, one tablespoon of mustard, mayonnaise, one tablespoon of chopped up parsley, some butter, and about a pound of cooked crab meat.

In a bowl mix the bread crumbs, egg, five tablespoons of mayonnaise, the parsley and scallions, and any seasoning you wish. Add the chopped up crab meat and mix it all together.

Make thin hamburger-style patties and fry in a pan greased with oil. If the mixture is too dry and doesn't hold together when you make the patties, add more mayonnaise.

Lacroix's Cream of Crab Soup

To make this delicious soup you will need: two hard-boiled eggs, flour, butter, ½ cup of whipping cream, milk, crab meat, and ¼ to ½ cup of sherry.

Mash up the two eggs until they are uniform in texture; if you have a food processor you can purée them. Mix in two tablespoons of flour, and a quarter stick of melted butter.

In a large pot mix the cream with about two cups of milk and heat it but do not boil. Add the egg and flour mixture and keep mixing it as you go.

Keep stirring as the soup cooks and add ¼ cup of sherry. Some versions of this soup use more sherry.

Remove the soup from the heat source and add the crab meat. Season with cayenne pepper to suit your taste!

⌒ SCALLOPS

Cleaning a scallop is easy. Pry open the shell and throw out everything except the white meat of the scallop. You'll need a couple of scallops for each of the following recipes.

Grilled Scallops

This is one of the quickest and easiest ways to cook scallops.

Put four (or more) scallops on a skewer and paint them with melted butter with a dash of garlic powder. Cook them on a grill until done (about two minutes on each side). One way to serve them is on a bed of wild rice.

Scallop Pasta

Cook as described above and then cut the scallops into quarters and mix with the pasta of choice!

Breaded Scallops

For this recipe you will need: flour, bread crumbs, a beaten egg, and some scallops.

Roll the scallop in flour, then dip it in the egg, and roll it in the bread crumbs. Don't worry if the scallop isn't completely covered with bread crumbs; the bread expands when you cook it.

Fry the scallops in a pan that has been lightly coated with oil.

Lorraine's Underwater Special

This recipe is for hardy souls only. It was shown to me by a fellow diver.

Find a scallop of legal size while diving. Pry it open and eat it. . . and offer some to your surprised dive buddy!

CHAPTER 11

Photography

Underwater photography is my personal favorite underwater activity! In many ways, techniques underwater photographers use are just the opposite of land photographers. For instance, a photographer in Africa photographing a dangerous animal such as a lion would most likely use a long telephoto lens to make the animal appear closer than it actually is. An underwater photographer, on the other hand, photographing a potentially dangerous animal such as a shark achieves the best results by using super wide-angle lenses to make the animal appear farther away than it really is.

COLOR ABSORPTION

One of the reasons underwater photographers like to shoot as close to their subjects as possible is color absorption. As light passes through water, various colors in the color spectrum are absorbed; reds are lost after the first 10 feet, followed by orange and green. By 100 feet everything takes on a bluish hue. The first time divers cut their hands underwater, they may be surprised by the greenish color of their blood!

Color absorption not only takes place vertically in the water column, but also horizontally. Even if you are using an underwater strobe, if you are more than 8 feet away from your subject, a substantial amount of light from the strobe will be absorbed before it reaches the subject. Using super wide-angle lenses allows you to shoot closer to your subject, which helps overcome the problem created by color absorbtion.

➤ EQUIPMENT

To be a competent underwater photographer requires an understanding of technique; you need to know what type of equipment to use to take the picture you want. Camera types vary from the inexpensive Instamatics, to the more expensive 35mm cameras with a variety of interchangeable lenses. As far as the serious amateur or professional photographer is concerned, there are basically two systems to choose from — The Nikonos system and the housed camera system.

The Nikonos System

The Nikonos V is the latest model in the Nikonos line. A new one with the standard 35mm lens will cost you about $550. It has an aperture priority system. This means that if you set the camera on automatic, you select the f-stop and the camera picks a shutter speed that will give the right exposure.

Since light bends when it passes from water to air (this is called refraction), *not all* Nikonos lenses can be used out of the water. This is because they have been optically corrected for use in water and distort objects if used out of the water.

You can take the Nikonos as it comes from the factory, jump in the water, and start taking pictures. Your pictures will improve dramatically as you add the various lenses and strobes that are available for the Nikonos. There are six lenses made by Nikon for the Nikonos. The 15mm is the top of the line (with a price tag of $1,500 with the viewfinder); the 20mm ($700 with viewfinder) is another excellent wide angle lens; the 28mm ($259) is a good second lens purchase choice. The 80mm ($260) is primarily an above-water lens, although it can be used in the water. Nikon also makes an above-water-only 28mm ($175) water-resistant lens.

The Housed System

A housed system involves taking a normal SLR 35mm camera and putting it in an underwater housing. The Nikonos is a range finder, which means there is a parallax problem when you compose your subject through the camera viewfinder (located above the lens). There is a difference between the view of the object as seen through the picture-taking lense and the separate viewfinder. With a housed camera, what you see through the viewfinder (and when you trip the shutter) is what you capture on film. This is painfully often not the case with the Nikonos.

Another advantage to a housed camera system is that you have an almost unlimited selection of lenses to choose from.

Some drawbacks to the housed system are its bulk; it definitely takes two hands to operate it. And generally speaking, housed systems are not as rugged as the Nikonos system. If you abuse your housed system you're in for an expensive problem. Within reason, the Nikonos is basically indestructible. Another consideration is that starting out with a housed system will cost you double what starting with a Nikonos will cost.

The Nikon F3 ($900 to $1,300) and the Canon F1 (about $800) are the two most often housed cameras. This doesn't mean you can't house an Olympus, a Pentax or a Minolta if you already own one. Ikelite makes plastic housings for these cameras and others. The cost of the housing will be in the $400 range. They will also make a housing for any camera on a custom basis. Many photographers prefer these lightweight housings. The camera goes in the housing without the motor drive, making the whole package lighter and smaller.

If you wish to house your camera with the motor drive attached, you'll need one of the heavy duty housings to handle the added weight. Prices ranges from $1,000 to over $2,000. You'll need two ports for the front of the housing. The ports on the front of the housing are what the camera's lens "sees" through, and generally most photographers get two of them. With macro lenses you'll use a flat port; while wide angle lenses require a dome port. The two macro lenses most used by photographers are the 55mm (about $300 for the Nikon), and the 105mm (about $600 for Nikon). Wide angle lens choices are limited only by what your camera manufacturer offers. Prices range from $1,500 (for the Nikon 15mm) and decrease in price for lenses with a larger millimeter length.

FILM

There are many types of film available to modern photographers. The first question is do you want to shoot prints or slides? I recommend you shoot slides. I still throw out a high percentage of every roll I shoot and this gets expensive with prints. You can always make prints later from your best slides.

Next, pick one type of film and stick to it. By doing this you'll learn what to expect as you re-experience certain lighting situations. I always use Kodachrome™ 64 (the chrome

The Nikonos V is a good camera to start taking underwater pictures with.

Some photographers prefer to house an above-water camera such as a Nikon F3.

This diver is holding a housed 16mm movie camera. Custom housings can be built for just about any camera made.

part of the name designates slide film) and generally I know what my f-stops will be in advance in certain situations.

How sensitive a film is to light is designated by its ASA number. The higher the number, the more sensitive the film is. If you are shooting in low light without a strobe, you'll want a high ASA. If you're shooting with a strobe or in bright light, you'll want a low ASA. One disadvantage that comes with high ASA films is they are grainy, which translates into a less sharp picture.

I recommend you use Kodachrome™ 64 (if you're using a flash). One reason is that if you plan to sell your pictures, most editors prefer Kodachrome™.

Some underwater photographers use Ektachrome, which

If you can't get near your subject, you may choose to shoot with available light, as was done with this shot of divers descending onto an airplane wreck.

tends to have a bluish hue to it. I don't care for that since blue is already a predominate color underwater. It's a personal judgment though — you might love it. Experiment a bit, and when you find a film you like, stick to it.

➴ AVAILABLE LIGHT

Taking pictures with available light is a good way to start in underwater photography since you'll only have the camera to contend with. The key to achieving good results is to take pictures of objects that lend themselves to available light photography. If you try to take a picture (without a flash) of a colorful sponge in 100 feet of water you probably won't like the results. But, if you shoot a silhouette of a diver in front of the sun, you should achieve pleasing results. Realize also that if you're trying to recreate a picture taken with a 15mm lens, and you're using a 35mm lens, it's not going to happen.

When shooting with available light, stay shallow; this will help minimize color loss. Also, position your subjects so they're facing into the sun to take full advantage of the light.

Get as *close* as you can to your subjects. This will again help minimize color loss. Be careful not to block the light. Before taking a picture, check where the sun is and position both your subject and yourself to take advantage of it.

When taking pictures of divers, try to position them over a light colored bottom (such as coral or sand) for contrast. This will help with color separation. The idea is to not have them blend in with their surroundings. A blue wetsuit tends to get lost against a blue background.

Before you take the picture, decide which part of the picture is most important as far as exposure. Get the lens as close to the object as it will focus and take a light reading with shutter set on automatic (F5.6 is a good place to start). The camera may indicate a different shutter speed than if you take a reading of the entire scene. If so, manually set the shutter to the speed indicated when you took the reading up close; this will help to ensure that your subject receives the correct exposure.

Silhouettes

To shoot silhouettes, take a light reading a few feet to the side of the sun and set your camera for this exposure. Have

Photographing models and other "top-side" subjects isn't practical with the Nikonos. If you like taking pictures out of the water, you may want to house a conventional SLR camera.

The Nikonos's 28mm lens is ideal for mid-size subjects such as this sea lion.

your subject swim across your field of vision and then take the picture when he is in between you and the sun.

If the camera's meter tells you to set the shutter at $\frac{1}{250}$ take two more pictures, one with the shutter set at $\frac{1}{125}$ and one at $\frac{1}{500}$. This is called bracketing. What you've done is taken one picture a little underexposed and one a little overexposed, along with the one that the camera meter thinks is right on. One of these should be to your liking.

You can also shoot silhouettes without shooting into the sun. Just take a light reading into the light, which will give you a good exposure for "the blue background." Then have your diver (or animal) swim into that space. Since they'll almost certainly be darker than the surrounding water, you should get a pleasing result.

Once you edit your first few attempts, you'll start to know what exposures work and under what circumstances—using the same film with the same ASA ratings of course!

➤ FLASH PHOTOGRAPHY

Using a flash with your camera will restore color lost from water absorption. One of the most important ingredients in producing attractive pictures while using a flash is the ability to balance ambient light with light from your flash. This means that if the surrounding light gives a light reading of F/5.6, you then set your strobe to expose also for f/5.6.

Wide Angle TTL

TTL means Through The Lens metering. When you turn a strobe on—assuming it's attached to the camera—the camera's shutter locks into a specified speed. You need to know what this speed is ($\frac{1}{90}$ with the Nikonos V) to balance successfully your photographs with TTL. Set your light meter at the shutter speed specified, and take a light reading to the side of your subject. Then set your f-stop to the indicated number (say f/5.6). Now when you take the picture, the camera will turn the strobe off when it has given enough light for an exposure of f/5.6. Since this matches the light behind the subject (where the strobe doesn't reach), the two light sources are balanced.

You can do the above procedure without a light meter as

follows. Turn the flash off and take a light reading with the camera's shutter set on automatic. Look through the viewfinder and turn the f-stop until you see the camera's sync speed displayed. For example, the Nikon F3 syncs at $\frac{1}{80}$ of a second. With the camera set on auto, both $\frac{1}{125}$ and $\frac{1}{60}$ will light up when the right f-stop has been hit. Now turn your flash on and take the picture.

Skin tones are one area of potential trouble when balancing with TTL. There is often a one stop difference between a diver's light colored skin and the rest of the picture area. The camera exposes for the larger dark area, often overexposing the lighter skin tones. The solution is to bracket with the camera's film speed dial by doubling the film speed. Housed TTL cameras usually have an ASA dial on the outside of the camera for this. For example, if you were shooting with a 100 ASA film, setting the camera's ASA dial to 200 makes the TTL meter think the film is more sensitive to light, and so it turns the flash off sooner.

Wide Angle Non TTL

Balancing with a manual strobe is a bit more complicated. Say your strobe has a guide number of thirty and the ambient light reading is f/5.6. You need to divide thirty by a number that will equal 5.6 (or that will come close). In this case thirty divided by five equals six. Six is close enough to 5.6 to work. What this tells you is you'd need to hold the strobe 6 feet away to get an exposure of 5.6.

Unfortunately you'll most likely be taking the picture closer than 6 feet away. Fortunately, most strobes have two or three power settings and each has its own guide number. Let's say the above strobe had a guide number at half power of fifteen. Fifteen divided by three equals five. That means at 3 feet with the strobe at half power you get an exposure of f/5, which is close enough to balance with the ambient reading of f/5.6. You could then try for an exact match by holding the strobe a few inches back to cut down on exposure.

I know it sounds complicated, but after editing a few rolls of film, you'll start to know where to hold your strobe to balance with specific ambient readings.

Back Scatter

Back scatter is a term used to describe the illumination of particles (by the strobe) suspended in the water. The closer the strobe is in line with the camera's lens the worse the problem becomes. Placing your strobe off to the side of the camera lights the particles from a different angle (than the lens) and reduces the problem.

➤ NIGHT PHOTOGRAPHY

Most underwater photographers shoot with Kodachrome™ 64. Wide angle photography at night is one occasion where switching to faster film (higher ASA) may be called for.

There are two reasons:

1. Every time you double your film speed, you cut down your exposure by one f-stop. Let's say your film is rated 100 and you're shooting at f/8 with your strobe at full power. If you were to change to a film rated ASA 200, you would need to change your f-stop to f/11 (assuming the strobe output is the same). Using a larger f-stop increases the depth of field. This gives you more leeway when focusing.

2. A higher rated film can also be used to help out underpowered strobes. Let's say you're using a TTL strobe and you're shooting at f/5.6; after every shot your strobe indicates that it has fired at full power, or has been unable to supply sufficient exposure. Switching to f/4 or f/2.8 would most likely remedy the situation, but would make focusing at night hard due to the limited depth of field. Using a faster film (and not changing the f-stop) lessens the amount of exposure needed from the strobe. If you were to switch from ASA 100 to ASA 400, your strobe could give f/5.6 (ASA 400) the same exposure it would have previously given f/2.8 (ASA 100). Remember, every time you double the ASA, you cut exposure by one stop.

You can increase your film's ASA without actually changing to the higher rated film, although quality suffers. In other words, you can shoot film rated ASA 100 at ASA 400. This is called "pushing" the exposure.

What you do is reset your camera's ASA dial to the desired speed. Each time you double the film's speed is referred to as pushing it a stop. When you take the roll to be processed, tell the lab how many stops you pushed it; 100 ASA shot at 400 is pushed two stops, etc. It's important to remember to tell them or the roll will come out underexposed.

Strobes

When shooting at night, the use of two strobes is highly recommended. A single strobe produces long, harsh shadows. Imagine shining a flashlight on someone in a pitch dark room —the shadow produced from the single light source is exaggerated because there isn't any ambient light. Pictures taken with a single strobe at night can look like that. The use of two strobes helps correct the problem since each strobe cancels the opposite strobe's shadow.

Don't panic if you only own one strobe, you can still get excellent results. To make the shadows less noticeable, place your strobe about 2 feet over the camera's lens. This will put the shadow behind your subject, making it less noticeable. It's a trade-off between lighting up the back scatter (which positioning the strobe like this will do) and eliminating the shadow.

Experiment to see what works best for your situation!

Silhouettes—such as this shot of a diver above the bow of a wreck—are a type of picture you can take if you don't own an underwater flash.

Focusing

If you can't see it, you can't focus on it. This is a problem at night.

There are two solutions. One, you can preset your focus, at 4 feet for example, and only take pictures at that range. Although this is limiting, it will force you to look for specific subjects, which usually produces better results than just swimming around and taking pictures of "anything."

A better solution is to use a modeling light. A modeling light supplies enough light to let you focus and compose your shots at night. They come in two forms, a built-in part of the strobe, or small flashlights strapped on top of the strobe. A hand-held flashlight won't work because both hands are needed to hold and operate the camera.

Another advantage to a modeling light is that it may eliminate the need for an underwater flashlight. It depends on where you're diving. Off the California coast, visibility can be less than 10 feet, and the water temperature is often in the 50's. Safety dictates a powerful flashlight. Off Palau on the other hand, the visibility exceeds 100 feet, and the water temperature averages 85 F . In those conditions, a modeling light may be more than adequate to see at night.

OTHER CAMERA CONTROLS

You'll also need a way to see the other controls on your camera and strobes. This is less important with a housed camera, since most of the needed information is illuminated inside the viewfinder. With the Nikonos, however, you'll most likely want a light to see the various controls.

Hand-held flashlights don't work because you need one hand to hold the camera and the other hand to make the adjustment. One solution is to strap, tape, or stick a Chemlight in your wetsuit sleeve (at the wrist). Chemlights are plastic tubes filled with glow-in-the-dark chemicals. They come in different colors and supply enough light to enable you to see the camera's controls.

Slave Strobes

Slave strobes can be fired in sync with your camera system without being attached to the camera. This is accomplished with the help of a sensor, usually located in the strobe's flash head. Some slaves can also be attached to a cable that has a sensor at the end.

When you push the camera's shutter, the primary strobe—the one attached to the camera—fires. The slave strobe's sensor then "sees" the flash from the primary strobe and fires the slave.

Since these strobes can be held or placed almost anywhere, they are extremely helpful to photographers working in any situation where ambient light is nonexistent.

Anytime you see a picture of a diver holding a flashlight, odds are he (or she) is actually holding a slave strobe. Give your subject a slave strobe and have him hold it as he would a flashlight. When you take the picture, the slave will fire, producing the illusion of a flashlight. Make sure the slave isn't pointing directly at the camera, and/or set the slave at quarter-power.

Divers holding slave strobes can be used to fill up areas of a picture that would otherwise be blank. Find a subject you can shoot at minimum focus, such as coral growths on the bow of a wreck. Compose the shot vertically, leaving the top third of the frame empty. Give two divers slave strobes and ask them to swim through the shoot about 10 feet in front of you. The divers and their "flashlights" add a second point of interest to the picture.

You can back light with a slave strobe by placing it behind your subject; this can produce very dramatic results. To avoid overexposing, place the slave three times as far from the camera lens as the primary strobe is from the subject. You'll get the distances nailed down after you edit your first couple of rolls.

A note on working with models, assistants, and slave strobes: You have to plan the shot before you get in the water. If everybody simply jumps in the water, enthusiasm and slave strobes in hand, you most likely won't get the shot, although you will have fun watching the confusion! It helps to draw a sketch before the dive to show people where to position themselves. You also need to show them where to point the strobes in relation to the camera. Of course, in diving there are no absolutes. If, after planning your shot, you go down and find killer whales feeding on white sharks, by all means abandon your plan and take a picture. . .and then get out of the water!

CHAPTER 12

Dive Travel

Many people only go scuba diving when they are on vacation. It may be that they specifically go on "a dive" vacation, or they may simply do a few dives while on a family vacation.

Some people don't like diving in their hometown because the water is cold. If you live in Minnesota, for example, diving in the winter would first require cutting a hole in the ice!

Some things to consider when planning a dive vacation include:

1. Hotel Location: Is the hotel on the beach? Or inland? If it is inland, you will have to commute to where the dive boat picks you up everyday. This may not be a problem since many dive operators pick up their clients at no additional charge. It is a consideration, however, for non-diving family members (and for you) who may not be diving. A long walk or taxi ride to the beach may not be desirable.

If the hotel is isolated and does not offer a variety of in-house restaurants, long drives to town may be waiting for you at the end of the day. When booking your trip, ask your travel agent where the hotel is located in reference to restaurants, beaches, shops, and the dive departure area.

For some people an isolated hotel may be desirable. If you're a newlywed couple for example, you may want to be isolated from crowds during your non-diving hours.

2. Hotel Versus Live-aboard: Live-aboard refers to a dive boat that you live on during your vacation. The advantage is that the boat can travel to lots of different dive sites, which gives you the opportunity to dive a variety of areas. The disadvantage is that basically all you are going to do is dive—

which is *my* idea of heaven! But for the non-diving members of your group, this may be *their* idea of hell! A live-aboard situation is really only for divers who want to maximize their time underwater.

Staying at a hotel, on the other hand, gives you the freedom to pursue a multitude of other activities in addition to diving. If one or two dives a day is enough, and you want to spend some time exploring, shopping, windsurfing, playing tennis, and horseback riding, then a live-aboard may not be for you.

3. Passports and Visas: Some destinations require visitors to obtain a special visa to enter the country. In addition, you may also be required to apply for a dive permit. Basically, this is just a way of keeping track of how many divers visit each year—and a way of supplying an additional source of tourist income.

Some countries, such as the Bahamas, only require proof of citizenship from U.S. citizens. A driver's license or birth certificate may be used in lieu of a passport. Personally, however, I recommend that you always travel with your passport. When in doubt check with your travel agent before departing.

4. Transportation: Nothing can ruin a vacation quicker than arriving at your destination only to discover that your dive gear was accidentally sent to the Sahara Desert!

Flying direct (with your luggage on the same plane) will help to eliminate the risk of your bags being placed on the wrong connecting flight. When booking your trip, ask if it is

If you travel with non-divers you may want a resort that offers other activities such as windsurfing.

possible to fly direct. While this may cost more, ultimately it may be worth the added expense.

If you must make connecting flights, check your bags only one flight at a time and carry them to your connecting flight. This reduces the risk of your bags becoming lost in transit.

Destinations frequented by divers sometimes have a higher risk of dive gear being stolen in and around airports. Putting your gear in a non-dive bag, such as a suitcase, reduces the chance of your gear being stolen since it is no longer recognizable as dive gear. Cameras, computers, and other valuable or fragile equipment are best carried on board to avoid possible theft and/or damage.

5. Insurance: There are two types of insurance the traveling diver should consider. First, insuring your gear against loss, theft, or damage is always a good idea. Losing your camera gear in an airport is a miserable experience, but you will be a lot more miserable if you didn't spend the few extra dollars it takes to insure it.

The other type of insurance is trip insurance. Imagine spending hundreds of dollars (or thousands) for a vacation only to have the trip cancelled the day before departure because of a hurricane. By purchasing trip insurance, you are guaranteed a refund if your plans are altered by unforeseen natural forces.

6. Local Customs: It is a good idea to read about local customs. For example, in some areas of the world a woman wearing a mini-skirt may be offensive to local sensibilities. Once while working on a film in Turkey, one of the women in our crew wore a mini-skirt that incited the locals to throw rocks at her.

Of course this is an extreme example of what could happen, but nonetheless it is a good idea to look into local customs.

7. Vaccinations: Some destinations may require special vaccinations. Malaria, for example, is a concern on some islands in the South Pacific. Check with your travel agent and doctor to determine what specific shots you may need.

8. Other Medical Considerations: Does the resort you are traveling to have a recompression chamber nearby? Don't take for granted that because an island is primarily known as a diver's resort that a recompression chamber is available.

Medical transportation can be very expensive. Helicopter evacuation, in particular, is costly. I recommend that you join The Divers Alert Network, more commonly known as DAN.

DAN offers insurance for medical evacuation as well as a host of other services. One useful service is a twenty-four hour dive accident hotline. It allows physicians (or divers) to call in with questions relating to dive accidents. If you injure yourself while diving in a lake in Kansas, the local doctor may not be familiar with dive-injury medicine. He can call DAN to speak with a doctor specializing in dive injuries, describe your symptoms, and get immediate expert advice on what to do. DAN's address is:

Diver's Alert Network
P.O. Box 3823
Duke University Medical Center
Durham, NC 27710
Phone: (919) 684-2948

They are open Monday through Friday 9-5 (EST). For emergencies only call the twenty-four hour Emergency Line: (919) 684-8111.

At the time of publication the cost for a one year membership is $40.

9. Bring What You Need: If you are going to spend hard-earned money to travel to some remote part of the world to go scuba diving, you don't need to get there only to discover that you did not bring your regulator and that the resort does not rent them. If you do not have your own dive gear, *make sure* that the resort positively rents dive gear and has enough on hand.

It is a good idea to bring backup gear if you have it. On a recent trip to the outer islands of Vanuatu, a woman in our dive group lost her mask while doing a back roll out of the Zodiac. Fortunately, another diver had two extra masks and was able to loan her one for the remainder of the trip. On the same trip another person did not bring a BC and was counting on renting one from the boat (we were on a live-aboard). Unfortunately, the boat did not rent gear and this person had to count on the generosity of other people to loan her their BC's while they weren't diving.

A few questions and phone calls made by your travel agent will help ensure that these problems don't happen to you.

In addition to dive gear, you should also bring toiletries, batteries, and any other items critical to the enjoyment of your vacation.

10. Purchasing Power: A few years ago some friends and I were on the island of Bonaire, off the coast of Venezuela, when Eastern Airlines filed for bankruptcy. Unfortunately, Eastern had failed to give the commuter airline that flew from Miami to Bonaire the money we had paid Eastern Airlines for our tickets.

When we went to the airport to depart, the ticket agent said, "Your tickets are worth as much as toilet paper." (Yes, this is a quote.) For those of us with credit cards or other means of purchasing new tickets, the situation was only an annoyance. Some other people, however, were stranded. When traveling, it is a good idea to have a little reserve money for emergencies.

11. Non-Diving Activities: If you are traveling with non-divers, you will want to find out what alternate activities the resort has to offer. Often one member of your family will dive, while others may prefer horseback riding or parasailing.

Don't assume that a hotel that advertises diving automatically also caters to non-divers!

⌁ WHERE TO GO

There is an almost endless list of scuba diving vacation spots. Here's a list of some of the more popular, along with a few of my personal favorites.

Palau

Palau is a ninety-three mile long chain of 328 islands in the South Pacific. With water temperatures averaging 86 degrees F. and visibility usually well over 100 feet, Palau is truly world class diving.

Palau is one of the most beautiful places I have ever been. If you are looking for a dive vacation and romantic getaway, this is the place.

Blue Holes is one of the more frequented dive sites in Palau. The "Holes" start 6 feet below the surface and tunnel down to about 130 feet (although it is possible to stay shallower), where they dump out on a wall.

Sitting at the bottom of one of the Blue Holes, watching it "rain" divers as they began their descent 130 feet above you is a memorable experience.

Another dive worth experiencing is a channel that was blasted through the center of a coral reef so boats could pass. Called *Wonder Channel,* the current is the attraction. Divers are dropped off at one end where the current carries them at a speed great enough that even holding onto a rock on the bottom is virtually impossible. You simply establish neutral buoyancy at your chosen depth—and then blast through the channel like a screaming locomotive—effortlessly. Once through the channel the boat retrieves the divers as they surface!

Ngemelis is probably Palau's best known wall dive. In my opinion this may be one of the best wall dives in the world!

The Palau Pacific Resort is an excellent hotel. Room service, restaurants, fresh water swimming pool, and other services allow non-divers also to enjoy time spent at the Palau Pacific. Their address is:

The Palau Pacific
P.O. Box 308
Koror, Palau, W.C.I. 96940
Phone: 600

Neco Marine runs an excellent dive service in Palau. Divers are picked up at a dock outside the Palau Pacific and shuttled to the various dive sites. Neco Marine's address is:

Neco Marine
P.O. Box 129
Koror, Palau, W.C.I. 96940
Phone: 325 or 206

As with any diver service, be sure to specify exactly what you want when making arrangements. If there are six people in your group and you want your own boat, be sure to tell your travel agent so that this can be arranged and confirmed in advance.

Bonaire

Bonaire is one of three islands in the Dutch Caribbean that are commonly referred to as the ABC Islands. Located roughly sixty-six miles off the coast of Venezuela, the other two islands are Aruba and Curacao. All three islands are visited by divers, but in my opinion Bonaire is the best.

One of the aspects I like about Bonaire is that it has terrific beach dives. Many dive resorts around the world offer unlimited beach diving as part of their package. Usually this means that you can get a tank any time of the day and do a dive off the beach in front of the hotel. The problem is that usually the beach in front of the hotel is so boring (underwater) that after one beach dive, you don't want to do another.

I stayed at Captain Don's Habitat and found the beach diving to be as enjoyable as the boat dives! Both the coral and fish life were as abundant and colorful as at sites that required twenty minute boat rides. Captain Don's address is:

Captain Don's Habitat
P.O. Box 333
Bonaire, Netherlands Antilles
U.S. Booking Office #: (800) 327-6700

Some of Bonaire's better-known dive sites would include: Ebo's Reef (known for black coral), Monk's Haven (known for the purple tube sponges indigenous to Bonaire), and Reppel.

Bonaire also offers activities for non-diving family members. The Salt Flats and large herds of pink flamingos are

This statue of a lady and a horse sits in 160 feet of water inside the wreck of the President Coolidge, *off Vanatu. World War II wrecks can be a major attraction for divers.*

both big tourist attractions. Two other hotels that attract large numbers of divers are The Sunset Beach Hotel, U.S. Booking Number: (800) 333-3484, and Sonesta Beach Resort, (800) SONESTA.

One word of caution when visiting Bonaire: Without proper protection you will be eaten alive by mosquitoes!

Catalina Island

Catalina lies twenty-six miles off the coast of southern California and is one of southern California's eight channel islands. The town of Avalon—with a year round population of 2500—is the only city on Catalina. Hotels, restaurants, shops, and a wide variety of activities make Catalina a favorite of tourists seeking a few days away from the pressure of city life.

Catalina is inexpensive to get to; cost of a round trip ticket by boat is about $30. If you travel to California, whether for business or pleasure, you may want to spend a few extra days diving Catalina.

Dive sites off Catalina offer something for divers of all skill levels. Newly certified divers will enjoy the calm, shallow bays along the front side of the island, while experienced divers may opt for deeper dives or shark diving adventures.

Some of Catalina's better known dive sites are:

The *Underwater Park* is located right in front of the Casino (not a gambling Casino, but a ballroom and a movie theater). The park is a buoyed-off area set aside exclusively for divers; it is a marine sanctuary and nothing living may be removed.

There are a couple of wrecks in the park. The *Sue–jack* lies in 90 feet of water and is a 60-foot long cement hulled ship. There is also an old glass bottom boat in 60 feet of water; a barge and other wreckage lie scattered in various other areas of the park. Marine life is abundant and fearless of divers.

Long Point is situated about midway down the front side of the island. The protected area inside the Point has lush kelp beds, rocky reefs, and flat sandy areas. The tip of the Point drops off into deep water and large pelagic animals from the deep sea are occasionally seen. Numerous movies and documentaries have been shot in this area because of the ideal conditions and abundant marine life.

Ship Rock is located off the Isthmus and is one of Catalina's best dive sites. Lush kelp beds and rocky reefs drop from the surface to 130 feet where a sandy bottom begins. Large populations of angel sharks can be found in the sandy areas, and a variety of marine life can be found in the rocky areas.

ARGO DIVING offers a variety of underwater adventures for divers visiting Catalina. Their address is:

ARGO DIVING SERVICES
P.O. Box 1201
Avalon, CA 90704
(213) 204-3650

The *King Neptune* is a 65-foot dive boat that takes divers out year round. They also run a number of hotels on the island and package deals can be had. Their address is:

The King Neptune
Catalina Diving Resorts
Dept. 1DBC
P.O. Box 1017
Avalon, CA 90704
(213) 510-2616

Truk Lagoon

Located in the South Pacific, Truk Lagoon is home to a ghost fleet of sixty-six Japanese ships that were sunk during a three day raid that took place in February of 1944. Truk Lagoon is world class diving at its best. Each ship would require dozens of dives to see everything it has to offer. I strongly recommend you do a little research on the ships in Truk before you go there—otherwise you could easily miss the dives that interest you the most!

Some of the better known wrecks at Truk are:

The *Shinkoku Maru*, at 504 feet, is the largest ship in Truk Lagoon. If only one dive is done on this ship the superstructure should be explored: cups, bottles, and other debris can be found scattered everywhere.

The hull of the ship is covered with soft coral growths and extends down to the sandy bottom at 130 feet. The wreck is home to a couple of gray sharks that add to the sense of adventure when diving this underwater World War II museum!

The *Nippo Maru* is one of my favorite wrecks in the Lagoon. A Japanese tank sits on its deck in 130 feet of

These stinging soft corals were photographed from less than 1 foot away with a super wide angle lens. Getting as close as possible to your subject helps eliminate color absorption and back scatter.

Most people are unaware that California has a species of hard coral. Taken at a site known as Fransworth Bank, off the back side of Catalina Island, this shot of Lorraine Sadler examining California Hydro Coral was made with a Nikonos V, with a 15mm lens and two strobes.

water-mines and their detonators can be found in the forward holds, while anti-tank guns lie scattered around the rear cargo holds. With all this hardware, it is easy to see why the *Nippo Maru* is an exciting wreck to dive.

The *Fijikawa Maru* is probably the most frequently visited wreck in Truk, and it may also be the most beautiful. There are two deck guns, one forward and one aft; ammunition, bottles, propellers, gas masks, and piles of other debris can be found in the cargo holes.

The *TRUK AGGRESSOR* (U.S. booking number (800) 348-2629) is a 120-foot live-aboard dive boat operating in Truk.

The Cayman Islands

These islands were discovered by Christopher Columbus in 1503 when he was accidentally blown off course during his fourth trip to the New World. Located south of Cuba and west of Jamaica, Cayman is actually made up of three islands: Grand Cayman is the largest and most commercially established, while Little Cayman and Cayman Brac are smaller and less developed.

Included among Grand Cayman's dive sites is *Stingray City*, named after the many stingrays that are routinely found there. The rays now expect to be fed and congregate under the dive boats that arrive on a daily basis; so you are pretty much guaranteed to see a large group of stingrays if you go there.

Eagle Ray Alley is a 30-foot deep canyon that runs along the face of the north wall. As the name implies, eagle rays are commonly sighted here.

New Tarpon Alley is a wall that begins in about 60 feet of water and drops off into the abyss, although certain areas bottom out on a shelf in about 150 feet of water. Tarpon are long silver fish that novice divers occasionally mistake for barracuda. Large schools of these fish are semi-routinely seen at this site.

Among Little Cayman and Cayman Brac dive sites worth noting: *Jackson Point* is known for stingrays in the shallow sandy areas and has typical Cayman wall-type diving at the drop off. *Bloody Bay Wall* is known for coral growths, large sponges, and its sheer drop off; the shallow area at the top of the wall is a good site for snorkeling.

I consider the Cayman Islands a good place to go if you

are traveling with non-divers. The diving is some of the best in the world and there are enough alternate activities for your non-diving companions to have an extremely enjoyable vacation.

One place you should be sure to visit is the *Turtle Farm* where hundreds of turtles are raised and kept in large pools. Some of the better known hotels include:

Don Foster's Dive
Phone: U.S. Booking #: (800) 83-DIVER

Cayman Brac Reef Beach Resort
U.S. Booking #: (800) 327-3835
Sunset House (on Grand Cayman)
U.S. Booking #: (800) 854-4747

Two of the better know live-aboard dive boats are:

The Little Cayman Diver
U.S. Booking #: (800) 458-2722

The Cayman Aggressor
U.S. Booking #: (800) 348-2628

Virgin Islands

The U.S. Virgin Islands are located forty miles east of Puerto Rico and are made up of the three islands—St. Croix, St. Thomas, and St. John.

St. Thomas is by far the most developed of the three islands and has a wide range of shops, restaurants, hotels, and night clubs. The harbor town of Charlotte Amalie is the hub of St. Thomas' activity and caters to international tourism.

St. John is the smallest and quietest of the three islands. It is only nine miles long and five miles wide. More than half the island has been designated a National Park.

The twenty-eight mile long island of St. Croix is the largest of the U.S. Virgin Islands and is made up of both tropical vegetation and desert-like dry lands.

Two miles off the northeast side of St. Croix lies Buck Island, which is home to a marine National Park. On the eastern end of Buck Island is an underwater nature course that is only open to snorkelers. With its shallow depths and identification plaques for the various species of coral, the nature trail is an excellent place to take non-diving group members to introduce them to the marine environment.

There are a number of excellent dive sites around Buck Island that can be enjoyed by divers while non-divers visit the underwater nature trail.

Other noteworthy sites around the U.S. Virgin Islands would include Congo Bay. With its colorful invertebrates, it is an excellent site for the macro-photographer. Wide angle photographers will occasionally find eagle rays, tarpon, and black-tip reef sharks in the deeper areas.

There are over fifty smaller diveable islands that surround the three main islands of St. John, St. Thomas, and St. Croix. Congo Bay is located off one of these islands, just north of the west end of St. John.

If you're looking for a beach dive while on St. Croix, then Butler Bay off the west end of the island may be your answer. The beach slopes off to about 25 feet, where a large variety of marine life can be found. You might want to do a second beach dive at Frederiksted Pier, located a ways south of Butler Bay. This site is said to be an exceptionally beautiful night dive.

French Cap Cay is located south of St. Thomas and St. John. With its elk horn coral, abundant marine life, and exceptional visibility, French Cap Cay is an great site for the wide angle photographer. The one drawback to this site is that it requires a longer boat ride to get to than most of the other dive sites.

The Sapphire Beach Resort is one of the many hotels on St. Thomas that cater to divers. Their address is:

Sapphire Beach Resort & Marina
P.O. Box 8088
St. Thomas, VI 00801
Phone (800) 524-2090

Three of the better known scuba tour operators on St. Thomas are:

Virgin Islands Diving Schools
Box 9707
St. Thomas, VI 00801
Phone (809) 774-8687

Underwater Safaris
Box 8469
St. Thomas, VI 00801
Phone (809) 774-1350

Joe Vogel Diving Co.
Box 6637
Charlotte Amalie
St. Thomas, VI 00801
Phone (809) 775-4320

If visiting St Croix try:

Christiansted
V.I. Divers, Ltd.
Pam Am Pavilion, Christiansted
St. Croix, VI 00820
Phone (800) 773-6045

Although not right on the water, the Hotel Caravelle caters
to divers. Their address is:

Hotel Caravelle
V.I. Divers, Ltd.
Pan Am Pavilion, Christiansted
St. Croix, VI 00820
Phone (800) 544-5911

On St. John, the Cruz Bay is one hotel that caters to divers
even though it is one street away from the water. They also
have their own fleet of dive boats. Their address is:

Coral gardens such as these are common off the islands of Palau.

Cruz Bay
P.O. Box 252
St. John, VI 00830
Phone (809) 776-6234

Cozumel

Cozumel is an island off the eastern tip of the Yucatan Peninsula in Mexico. The thirty-mile-long island is popular with divers from the United States who are seeking a tropical vacation at an affordable price. A week in Cozumel can cost you less than $1000—and that includes airfare! Cost aside, Cozumel has terrific diving. Wall diving is generally the rule, and all dives are drift dives.

Like Bonaire, Cozumel offers some better than average beach dives. The area around the La Ceiba Hotel offers some excellent beach dives for the novice and is often used for training purposes. Some of Cozumel's other better known sites are:

Colombia Reef, located at the southwestern end of Cozumel, is one of my personal favorites. Large coral towers separated by barren sandy areas and a sheer drop-off typify the area. As with most of the island's offshore sites, currents can be strong and unpredictable. I recommend you carry a

Children in Truk develop their swimming skills at an early age.

whistle or some other form of signaling device in case your boat fails to see you when you surface!

Maracaibo Reef is located south of Colombia Reef. Because of the long boat ride many of the half-day boats don't go there, so if you want to dive this site you should make arrangements in advance. The possibility of seeing big animals is what brings divers to Maracaibo Reef. Since it's situated in "open water," the chances of seeing sharks, a manta ray, or some other pelagic species are greater at this site. Keep in mind, however, that it's still a gamble...your long boat ride may or may not be rewarded. When I dove Maracaibo for example, the only things I saw were lots of coral and small fish.

The International Pier, just south of the La Ceiba Hotel, is an excellent site for the macro-photographer. Bright red sponges, coral growths, and a host of other invertebrates can be found growing on the cement pier pilings. The international pier is one of the best night diving sites (off the beach) Cozumel has to offer.

Palancar Reef is the best known site off Cozumel. Large coral towers and a sheer drop-off into the abyss make Palancar typify what Cozumel is known for. The reef runs parallel to the island and covers a large area. One area of the reef that should be visited is La Herradura, where the local divers have placed an underwater statue.

The La Ceiba Hotel is an excellent choice for divers. Their address is:

La Ceiba Hotel
P.O. Box 284
Cozumel, Mexico
(800) 777-5873

The Hotel El Presidente offers both bungalows and single hotel rooms and is situated on the water. Their phone number in Mexico is 2-03-89.

Two recommended dive operations in Cozumel are Aqua Safari's (Phone number is Cozumel 2-01-01) and Fantasia Divers (Phone number in Cozumel 2-07-80).

The Bahamas

More specifically, Nassau on New Providence Island has long been a tourist destination for divers and other tropical island vacationers. Gambling is legal on New Providence Island and many of the hotels have casinos as well as a host of other modern services.

Paradise Island is a narrow strip of land connected to the northeast end of New Providence Island. Large hotels, a convention center, and numerous shops and restaurants make this area the focus of much of the tourist activity.

Diving-wise, however, you may choose to stay at the west end of the island where boat rides to some of the deeper sites won't be as long. For example, Stuart Cove's Nassau Undersea Adventures, located at Lyford Bay on the west end of the island, offers shark diving adventures. Their address is:

Stuart Cove
Nassau Undersea Adventures
P.O. Box CB 11697
Nassau, Bahamas
U.S. Booking Number (800) 468-9876

Some other worthwhile sites around New Providence Island include:

Clifton Wall on the southwest end of the island can be dove by both novice and advanced divers. Depth ranges from 30 feet to over 5,000 feet in some areas. Various species of sponges and a steep drop-off make Clifton Wall a site worth revisiting.

The Sand "Chute" is actually part of Clifton Wall. A 40-foot wreck and some short tunnels in the reef are the attractions here!

Trinity Caves is one of the sites just off Paradise Island. As with many of the sites in this area, depth is in the 40-foot range. The site is a favorite of photographers due to the occasional grouper sighted and the large populations of lobsters found under the numerous ledges and small crevices in the area. The north side of New Providence Island is a marine preserve and nothing can be removed, so look but don't touch!

Numerous movies have been made on and around New Providence Island. Many of the wrecks deliberately sunk for filming purposes have now become artificial reefs that attract divers. The 100-foot freighter *Tears of Allah* was sunk for the James Bond film *Never Say Never* and sits in 50 feet of water south of Clifton Point.

Thunderball, another James Bond thriller, was shot nearby, where the remains of an jet airplane set remain. The LCD Landing Craft Wreck located in 20 feet of water south of Athol Island, just east of Paradise Island, was also used during the filming of *Thunderball.*

A Cessna 310 Airplane was also sunk in 50 feet of water off the east end of the island during the filming of *Jaws 3!*

The Willaurie is one of the larger wrecks in the area. This 130-foot mail boat was intentionally sunk in 1988 just south of Goulding.

The Divi Bahamas Beach Resort and Country Club on New Providence Island caters to divers. Booking information can be obtained by calling (800) 333-3484.

Sun Divers is an excellent dive operation on New Providence Island. Their address is:

Sun Divers
Box N 10728
Nassau, Bahamas
Phone (809) 325-8927

The other islands that make up the Bahamas chain are also worth visiting. The Underwater Explorers Society (UNEXSO) on Grand Bahama, for example, offers scuba diving adventures with wild dolphins! Information can be obtained by writing:

UNEXSO
P.O Box 5608
Ft. Lauderdale, FL 33310
Phone (809) 373-1244

⌒ TRAVEL AGENTS

When planning a dive vacation it's extremely beneficial to book your trip through a travel agent who specializes in scuba diving packages. A non-dive related agency probably won't have the latest information about resorts that are overbooking their boats, aren't giving advanced divers the freedom they desire, or are lacking some other service that could make the difference between having a fun trip—or a bad one.

If you have special needs or desires, such as a private boat for your group, advanced dives, or unique photography desires, tell the travel agent. A dive specialty agency can usually

Although often portrayed as dangerous, these schooling barracuda are of no threat to divers.

This mako shark is one of the ten or so species of shark that are considered dangerous to man. (Photo by Howard Hall.)

set these things up in advance.

Two agencies that cater specifically to divers are:

Sea Safaris
3770 Highland Avenue
Suite 102
Manhattan Beach, CA 90266
Phone (800) 821-6670

See & Sea Travel
50 Francisco Street
Suite 205
San Francisco, CA 94133
Phone (415) 434-3400
(800) DIV-XPRT

Chris Newbert's Rainbowed Sea Tour gives you the chance to travel to some of the best dive locations in the world, with one of the best underwater photographers in the world. If you're into photography, you should look into this operation. Chris Newbert leads all the trips personally and runs a first-class service. Rainbowed Sea Tours are, however, a bit pricier than some of the other operations. Information can be obtained by writing:

Rainbowed Sea Tours, Inc.
75-5751 Kuakini Highway, Suite 103
Kailua-Kona, HI 96740
Phone (800) 762-6827
(808) 326-7752
Fax (808) 329-8000

CHAPTER 13

Marine Life

Fear of marine life is probably one of the most common reasons people stay out of the water or don't want to try scuba diving. Television and films often portray the ocean's creatures as predatory, blood-thirsty animals that roam the seas *seeking* human flesh! Nothing could be further from the truth.

Educating yourself about marine life will increase your comfort level while diving since it eliminates the fear of the unknown. Many beginning dive students have a lot of apprehension about "what's down there?" If the thought of encountering a certain type of marine life makes you uncomfortable, obtaining facts about that animal may alleviate your fears.

Moray eels are a good example. Often portrayed as vicious, snake-like creatures with poisonous fangs and vise-like jaws, these animals are feared by many new divers. Morays are actually one of the most docile of animals. They are nocturnal and spend their days hiding in rocky crevices. Unfortunately, so do lobsters. When a diver gets bitten by a moray, it's usually from reaching into a hole to grab a lobster, unaware that the den is also shared by an eel. Imagine sneaking up to a sleeping dog you didn't know and reaching into his dog house, startling him . . . I imagine the result would be the same.

Another reason to learn about marine life is that it's fun to know what you're looking at while diving. When I see a species I've never seen before, it's exciting. Knowing exactly what I'm seeing makes the experience more enjoyable.

If you're planing to dive in an area you've never been to before, it's a good idea to look into what types of marine life you can expect to encounter. In a practical sense, it's a good

A sunfish (a.k.a. Mola Mola) swims in open water 30 miles off the coast of southern California.

idea to know if there are any poisonous species. Sightseeing-wise, knowing what to look for and where to look will help you get the most out of your time underwater.

Obviously, it would be impossible to cover every type of marine life you may encounter in one chapter, or in one book for that matter. Included here are the animals that people tend to be frightened of the most. In most cases you will find the fear is unjustified!

SHARKS

Of the roughly 350 species of shark, only about ten or so are known to attack man occasionally; the odds of a diver *seeing* one of these species unintentionally are pretty slim. In fact, if you do see a shark while diving, you are lucky! In my first fifteen years of diving off Southern California, I didn't see even one of the supposedly dangerous species of shark.

If you do encounter a large predator while diving—such as a great white shark—the chances of being attacked (in my opinion) are almost nonexistent. When sharks attack man, it's almost always by mistake. A surfer lying on a surf board, with his arms and legs hanging over the side, looks a lot like a sea lion to a hungry white shark swimming below. But a diver doesn't look like anything the shark is used to eating.

When sharks bite people, they often let go and swim away. Could it be that human flesh doesn't taste good to a shark? Think about it—you hear about shark attack victims "washing up on shore," but if a shark really wanted to eat someone . . . there wouldn't be anything left to wash up!

Moray eels have a reputation for being vicious, but are actually docile animals that bite only when provoked.

The colorful and beautiful lionfish is capable of delivering a painful sting, but fortunately is nonaggressive. When divers do get stung it's usually by accident, as a result of not looking where they're putting their hands. (Photo by Howard Hall.)

The point is...when a shark bites a person, it's by mistake; and you as a diver are less likely than a surfer or surface swimmer to accidentally look like a shark's food source.

Keep in mind, however, that if you're spearing fish or doing something that could attract and confuse a shark—then your chances of being attacked increase. Shark divers for example, who put food scent in the water and jump in when the hungry sharks show up, are more likely to be bitten.

STINGRAYS

Stingrays are not dangerous to divers unless you accidentally kneel, or step, on one. Most stingray "attacks" reported every year are the result of someone stepping on one just offshore; they're more of a threat to beachcombers than divers.

If you see a stingray while diving, don't fear it—it won't attack you. Rays spend much of their time in sandy areas, half-buried with only their eyes showing. If you see a pair of eyes sticking out of the sand, it may be a stingray—so don't "land" too close.

SCORPIONFISH

The scorpionfish (also known as the zebrafish or lionfish) is common in many of the world's tropical seas. Perhaps because they are related to the more poisonous stonefish,

This electric torpedo ray is capable of stunning its prey with an electrical shock. (Photo by Howard Hall.)

lionfish have a reputation among non-divers as being aggressive and dangerous. These fish have eighteen spines that are capable of delivering a venom that is known to be excruciatingly painful, but fortunately they are not aggressive towards divers. The only way you'll get stung is by not being aware of what your hands (or some other part of your body) are about to touch. If you do get stung, you're in for a miserable experience, but you'll probably survive.

Scorpionfish seem to just "hang out" in select areas of the reef. For underwater photographers, they make ideal subjects!

STONEFISH

I've never seen a stonefish while diving, and you probably won't either—even if you are diving within a foot of one. These fish are so well-camouflaged that spotting them can be next to impossible. Unfortunately that's also the perspective problem: if you can't see it, it's hard to avoid. If you're diving in an area that is known to be home to the stonefish—watch where you put your hands! *This one can kill you*, and make you incredibly miserable in the process.

People have survived being stung by a stonefish. South African icthyologist J. L. B. Smith was stung in 1950. He said of the incident, "Having being stabbed and stung by a stingray, it is possible to say the stonefish is in a class by itself."

There is an antivenin for the stonefish, but the chances of you and the antivenin being together when you get stung are slim . . . so watch where you put those hands!

MORAY EELS

Moray eels are one of the most docile creatures in the ocean, but for some reason endless myths abound about the moray's reputed viciousness!

One of the silliest is that a moray can't reopen its mouth if it bites something too big (like a human arm, the story goes). The teller of the story goes on to describe how you have to bring the eel to the surface to pry open its vise-like jaws. I've even overheard scuba instructors telling this one!

The fact is moray eels can let go of anything they bite into; I've seem them do it dozens of times. If you see a moray eel while diving, don't worry; it's not going to attack you.

A diver gently handles an octopus.

➤ BARRACUDA

Barracuda are another creature of mythical viciousness—I've swum in schools of hundreds of them without incident. Barracuda have "dog-like" teeth, which is probably what contributed to their reputation as a man hunter. Occasionally large schools will be rather fearless of divers and approach within a few feet. I think this is more a case of the diver being in the school's "swim path" than fish curiosity.

Barracuda are said to be attracted to shiny objects, so you might not want to wear necklaces, bracelets, earrings, etc. while diving.

One of the first times I saw a barracuda was on a night dive off the Cayman Islands. After a few minutes of following the fish around, I accidentally (because it was night and I couldn't see) cornered the animal in a canyon, blocking its only avenue of escape with my body. Naturally the frightened fish made a run at me. Not yet having any experience in these types of situations, I froze in fear as the barracuda flew by inches from my head. The moral of the story is don't be stupid when dealing with any type of marine life. Cornering a fish with sharp teeth and blocking its only escape path with my body was a dumb thing to do.

Think about your actions from the animal's perspective. Don't do anything that would make it feel threatened or force it to act defensively.

➤ ELECTRIC RAY

There are about thirty species of electric rays worldwide, and the amount of electrical shock they can generate varies from species to species. The shock-producing organs are located on each side of the animal's body and the rays can control their output at will.

If you see an electric ray while diving, don't get too close. It has to be fairly near to shock you, so if you give it enough room, you won't have a problem. I know of one diver in California who mistook one for an angel shark and tried to "pet" it. He described the sensation as similar to what he experienced when he stuck a knife in a toaster (no comment)!

↢ OCTOPUS

The octopus is another creature that has been incorrectly portrayed as dangerous predator that attacks divers and strangles them with blood-thirsty tentacles!

In actuality, octopi are gentle, shy creatures incapable of doing any damage to a diver. Most species are small—not much larger than a foot or two—and prey primarily on shellfish. There is a large species of octopi off the western border of the U.S. and Canada that averages 4 to 5 feet, but it too is of no threat to divers.

The blue ringed octopus is found in Australia and its bite *can* kill a man. Fortunately it is completely nonaggressive—and only about 4 inches long. When people have been bitten, it's usually because they were handling the animal.

↢ SEA SNAKES

Of the roughly fifty species of sea snakes, all are poisonous and capable of killing a human. Some marine biologists believe the venom from some species to be *fifty* times more deadly than that of the king cobra!

Fortunately, sea snakes are completely nonaggressive and don't "attack" people. It is estimated that only about 25% of the people bitten by sea snakes are actually poisoned. This may be because the snakes have such small mouths that they cannot easily bite a human unless they bite a finger or other small part of the human anatomy. Sea snakes hold and "chew" the venom into their prey, which also may account for why some people bitten by sea snakes aren't actually poisoned.

Sea snakes have lungs and breathe air; the first time you see one will probably be when it makes a swim for the surface to breathe. Give the snake the respect it deserves, and you won't have any problems.

↢ WHALES

If you see a whale underwater, you are an incredibly lucky person! Most divers I know have never had an encounter with a whale. If you and a whale do happen to cross paths unexpectedly, don't be scared. Whales don't eat people—so enjoy the experience!

CHAPTER 14

Fresh Water

If you don't live in a coastal city, your first dives will most likely be in a lake, rock quarry, spring, river, or some other fresh body of water. Fresh water diving basically only differs from salt water diving in the areas of buoyancy and depth gauge readings; the rest of your gear works exactly as it would in the ocean. You don't have to "relearn how to dive" if you're planning to dive in fresh water.

If you're going to be diving more than 2000 feet above sea level, however, there are some changes you need to make in how you use the dive tables; more on this matter later.

Some fresh water sites have the best visibility found anywhere in the world. Ginni Springs in High Springs, Florida, for example, is known for unbelievable visibility and attracts divers from around the world. One thing I like about diving in fresh water is not having to worry about the hassle of cleaning my gear after a day's diving. Salt water divers have to rinse their gear thoroughly after every dive, since salt water corrodes dive gear quickly if it is not cleaned.

Another reason to dive fresh water is to see marine life that is indigenous to the fresh water environment. Salamanders, turtles, trout, bass, crayfish, and a host of other animals will please both the sightseer and the photographer.

Fresh water diving affords you the opportunity to go diving if you are traveling inland away from the ocean. In many cases you may discover that you are the *first person* ever to dive a particular spot! Your chances of discovering something unusual—be it a Civil War relic, an unknown shipwreck, or just a previously undiscovered dive site—are greatly increased.

Another advantage to fresh water exploration is that fresh water doesn't corrode objects as quickly as salt water does. A wreck subject to ocean storms and the corrosive effects of salt water can be reduced to little more than a pile of rubble after a few years. Fresh water wrecks are often in better condition than those wrecks found in salt water.

➤ TYPES OF FRESH WATER ENVIRONMENTS

Lakes

A lake is defined as a large inland body of standing water. Many of the hazards that divers encounter in the ocean are also present in some of the larger lakes around the world. The Great Lakes (Lake Superior, Lake Michigan, Lake Huron, Lake Erie, and Lake Ontario) are so large that the only difference between them and the ocean is the fact that they are fresh water. Surf, currents, and other dangers found in any ocean (because of their size) are the same.

Rivers

A river is defined as a natural stream of water of considerable volume. The main consideration/danger when diving in a river is the current. Quite a few divers (and swimmers) have been injured or drowned from underestimating a river's current! If you are planning to dive a river, check with a local dive store for advice about what areas of the river are safe to dive and in what areas hazards may exist.

Springs

A spring is defined as a source of water that comes from the ground; one thing springs are often known for is terrific visibility. A potential hazard present at many springs is an abundance of underwater caves. Wakulla Spring in Wakulla County, Florida, for example, is a maze of underwater tunnels that go back thousands of feet—many of which have yet to be explored. Because of the obvious risk in this type of environment, divers are often banned from some springs. *Do Not Under Any Circumstances Ever Enter An Underwater Cave Unless You Have Obtained Competent Instruction And Are Using The Required Specialty Equipment!*

Quarries

A quarry is defined as an open excavation. In some areas of the world an old rock quarry that has filled up with water may be the only diveable body of water available. One possible hazard at many quarries is the presence of old excavation equipment. The equipment may present an entanglement or some other type of hazard, so divers should be cautious at all times. Ironically, what may make quarries hazardous is also what makes them interesting. The fact that man once inhabited the area increases the likelihood of finding unusual souvenirs from your dive. The excavation equipment often gives a "wreck dive" feel to rock quarry dives.

Dams

A dam is defined as a barrier that confines a flow of water. Dams offer some unusual hazards to underwater explorers. Often a dam may have an underwater drain or "run-off." If a diver is in the vicinity of one of these run-off valves when it is opened, the suction created would be overpowering and could pin a diver underwater with very little chance of getting free. I once dove a pond in Vermont that had been created by damming up a stream; at one end of the pond was what literally looked like a giant bathtub drain plug, which would enable the pond to be drained if need be. If you ever encounter something like this *do not* attempt to open, pull free, or in any way tamper with an unusual looking valve, drain, or any other unidentified mechanical device.

Some dams offer unusual underwater exploratory opportunities! Like rock quarries, dams are often flooded areas that were once inhabited by man. Unusual souvenirs and other strange items are often encountered in dams. It is rumored, for example, that an Indian village sits at the bottom of Lake Isabella (in California), which was created by damming the Kern County River.

Ponds

A pond is a small body of still water. Ponds usually have the advantage of having absolutely no current, in addition to the fact they're so small that getting lost underwater isn't a consideration.

Keep an eye out for fishing lures (in any fresh water environment) that may have been torn loose or lost by past fishermen. Hooks, lures, and old fishing line are potentially hazardous to divers; they also make nice souvenirs. I have a large collection of unique lures obtained during a two week diving tour of New England.

Streams

A stream is basically a small river. Usually they are not deep enough to dive in, but if you find one that is, the same precautions mentioned about rivers should be practiced in streams.

Waterfalls

I don't imagine that anybody would be silly enough to attempt to go diving under a waterfall or to go diving above a waterfall, but if you are, realize that life can get extremely hazardous at the bottom of a waterfall! The force of the water is capable of pinning a diver to the bottom, making it virtually impossible to surface. If you should find yourself in this predicament, the only solution is to crawl along the bottom towards shore, or to crawl downstream until free of the force of the waterfall. Basically though, don't go diving anywhere near a waterfall!

BUOYANCY

Salt water weighs 64 pounds per cubic foot; fresh water only weighs 62.4 pounds per cubic foot. So, fresh water isn't as dense, nor does it weigh as much as salt water. Since a diver displaces the same amount of water in fresh water as he does in salt water, he is more negatively buoyant in fresh water (Archimedes' Principle, see Chapter 5). Generally, you want to remove about 3% of your weight belt for fresh water diving. This is only a reference point, you may need to remove more or less weight for your particular situation.

ALTITUDE

Many lakes are above sea level, and special considerations must be made when diving at high altitude. As you ascend above sea level, atmospheric pressure decreases; at sea level atmospheric pressure is generally 14.7 psi, but at 7,000 feet, for example, it is about 11.34 psi. This means that at the end of your dive you are under less pressure, so nitrogen bubbles are free to expand to a larger size than what standard dive tables are calculated on. The higher up you go, the more pronounced this problem becomes.

Arriving at Altitude

When you arrive at an altitude above sea level, you should consider yourself in a repetitive dive group before you even enter the water; this is because the reduced atmospheric pressure allows nitrogen bubbles in your blood to expand. NAUI (their address is below) sells literature that will tell you what your repetitive dive letter (from the dive tables) is upon arrival at various altitudes.

The procedure is to treat any dive made within twelve hours of your arrival at any altitude above sea level as a repetitive dive.

Depth Gauge Correction

Depth gauges are calibrated, or zeroed in for use at sea level. When you take them to altitude, they are no longer a reliable source of depth information. One solution is to buy a gauge that has an elevation correction dial (Tekna makes one). These depth gauges allow you to manually set the depth gauge needle to "zero" before your dive. If you are going to do a lot of diving at altitude, I recommend you purchase this type of gauge.

Depth gauges sense water weight, so it will take more fresh water to equal the same depth reading in salt water (since fresh water weighs less than salt water). For exact depth readings, you should add about 3% to what the gauge reads while underwater.

Dive Tables

Because of the reduced atmospheric pressure at altitude and because fresh water weighs less than salt water, standard U.S. Navy Dive Tables *cannot* be used. You need to get a set of tables calibrated for the altitude at which you will be diving.

NAUI sells an excellent book about diving at altitude, which has a complete set of conversion tables for up to 14,000 feet. NAUI's address is:

NAUI
P.O. Box 14650
Montclair, CA 91763-1150

Computers

There are a couple of dive computers on the market that are capable of functioning above sea level. Using a computer is one way of avoiding the hassle of recalibrating the tables. If you think you will be doing a lot of diving above sea level, you might want to look into a computer (see Chapter 15 for more on computers).

Jelly Fish Lake in Palau is filled with jelly fish that have lost their ability to sting.

CHAPTER 15

Dive Computers

Dive computers can increase your diving safety tremendously. What the computers do is electronically monitor the amount of nitrogen your body is absorbing while diving. The computers are more effective than standard dive tables since they are "dynamic"; in other words, they travel with the diver as he ascends and descends in the water column. Standard dive tables are rigid, and calculate a dive based on the deepest depth obtained during the dive. Imagine a diver who descends to 90 feet for five minutes, and then ascends to 30 feet for fifteen minutes. The dive tables would calculate the dive as a 90-foot dive for twenty minutes, while the computers credit the diver for the shallower time spent at 30 feet. The end results are longer dives and shorter surface intervals. Divers using standard dive tables spend less time underwater than divers diving with computers.

COMPUTER TERMINOLOGY

In order to use a computer safely while diving, it is helpful to understand some of the theory on which the manufacturers base their calculations.

Periodically in dive computer literature, you will come across the term "model." "Model" refers to a set of mathematical calculations used to determine how fast various body tissues absorb nitrogen. Also included in the "model" profile is how fast body tissues release nitrogen.

Nitrogen absorption and release is often referred to as "ongassing" and "outgassing." As most divers understand, "ongassing" occurs more rapidly the deeper a diver is. "Out-gassing" begins when a diver reaches shallower depths. For this reason most computers are based on "multilevel" dive profiles.

Tissue half-times refer to how quickly a tissue absorbs nitrogen. If a tissue has a half-time of five minutes, it means it would take five minutes for that tissue to become 50% full. After an additional five minutes has passed, the remaining half tissue would also become 50% full. In other words after ten minutes the tissue is 75% full. Each five minute period is referred to as a half-time. After 6 half-times the tissue is 98.4% full. Since this is so close to 100%, a tissue is said to be full after six half-times. In this example a tissue with a five minute half-time would be considered full (or saturated) after thirty minutes.

The same theory works in reverse when calculating how long it takes a tissue to completely outgas. The above tissue with the five minute half-time would take thirty minutes, or six half-times ($6 \times 5 = 30$), to completely outgas.

"M values" refer to how much nitrogen a tissue can absorb before a diver is at risk of becoming bent if he were to ascend directly to the surface. M values are stated in feet-of-seawater (FSW). For example, at sea level atmospheric pressure is equal to 33 feet of seawater. Air is made of roughly 79% nitrogen...so to obtain the M value at sea level, multiply 33 (FSW) by 0.79, which equals 26 feet of seawater. When a diver has reached the no-decompression time limit while underwater, at least one of his body tissues has reached its M value.

The various tissues in the human body absorb nitrogen at different rates. Body tissues that have a high circulation of blood flowing through them absorb and outgas nitrogen faster than tissue with poor blood flow. Bone marrow is a "slow" tissue, while the brain is "fast" tissue. A fast tissue may have a half-time of five minutes, while a slow tissue may have a half-time of over 400 minutes.

Dive tables are based on tissue half-times of five minutes to 120 minutes. Some computers assign slow tissue half-times of 480 minutes. This is one reason why the computers are often considered more "conservative" than dive tables.

COMPUTER FEATURES

On/Off Switches

Most computers are turned on in one of three ways.

Manual switches are simply knobs or levers that are turned by the user prior to a day's dive. The disadvantage is that you can accidentally turn the unit off between dives. On a recent dive vacation, I was horrified to find one of the boat's deck hands curiously flipping the on/off switch of my computer back and forth! When the unit is turned off all prior dive/nitrogen absorption information is erased. The advantage is that you can turn the unit on and off when you want to conserve battery life.

Immersion switches are the most convenient because they automatically turn the computer on when it gets wet. The obvious advantage is that it eliminates the possibility of forgetting to turn the computer on before you dive. The disadvantage is that some of the computers take a few moments to perform their "self diagnostic tests" once turned on and will not function properly if you begin your dive before they have completed this start-up procedure. One solution is to wet the computer prior to entering the water.

Scuba tank/pressure-activated switches are another convenient on/off switch. These units are connected directly to the first stage of your regulator and are turned on automatically when you turn on your air and pressure enters the system. These units also do duty as submersible pressure gauges, which cuts down on the number of gauges you need to take in the water with you.

Power Source

The main considerations with computer power sources are battery life span, if you can change the battery without losing information stored in the computer, and if there is a low battery warning/indicator.

Some computers require that they be sent back to the manufacturer to have their batteries changed. The advantage is usually incredibly long battery life, so you don't need to worry about changing it very often. The disadvantage is it's a drag to have your computer go down while on vacation in the middle of the South Pacific.

Some computers have batteries that the user can change. Some computers have a battery life of only a few days while others last for hundreds of hours. The advantage is that you can change your battery yourself without the inconvenience of having to send it back to the manufacturer. The disadvantage is that there is a slight risk of flooding the unit due to improper maintenance or failing to seal the unit correctly after a battery change.

Depth Gauge

All computers have some type of depth gauge. Most have a digital readout of your current depth and some also have a type of graph that also gives depth information.

Some computers also have a maximum depth indicator that allows you to see what the deepest point of your dive was/is at a glance.

Bottom Timer

All computers feature some type of bottom timer to keep track of how long you are submerged. Most also have a read-out that tells you what your remaining no-decompression time is at your current depth. This is a really useful feature and allows you to maximize your bottom time.

Surface Interval Time

Most computers tell you how long you have been out of the water. This is useful information when planning repetitive dives. It is also useful if you accidentally do get bent since it will accurately tell medical people how much time has passed since your last dive.

Memory

Memory refers to how many past dives the computer stores and displays. This also is a useful feature if you should suffer from decompression sickness.

No-Decompression Times for Repetitive Dives

This is a scrolling feature that tells you how long you can

stay down for a dive you are about to make without exceeding no-decompression limits. Depth is displayed along with its current no-decompression time. Usually the display will start at 30 feet and scroll to 130 feet or so.

What is good about this feature is the computer recalculates the no-decompression times as your surface interval increases. This eliminates having to calculate repetitive dives on conventional dive tables. You simply look at your computer, wait for it to display the depth you plan to go to, and then read the no-decompression time readout.

This feature is recommended because it eliminates accidents caused by mistakes made while making calculations with conventional dive tables.

Temperature

Some computers have a current temperature readout. These can often be obtained in either Fahrenheit or Celsius readouts and are not considered critical to dive safety.

Tank Pressure

Computers that are connected directly to the first stage of your regulator also have a built-in submersible pressure gauge. These are easier to read than analog gauges since they give you a digital readout. In other words, instead of knowing you have slightly less than 1500 psi left (with an analog gauge), the computer's SPG tells you that exactly 1320 psi is left.

How Long Your Air Will Last

This feature tells you how long (usually in minutes) your air will last at your current depth. For example, you're swimming along at 90 feet. You look at your computer, it tells you that you have 1700 psi left, and you will be out of air in twenty-two minutes. This obviously is useful information to the diver.

Low Battery Power Indicator

As the name implies, this lets you know when the computer's battery is approaching the end of its life. It avoids computer failure due to loss of power and is a recommended feature.

Rate of Ascent Indicator

Most computers have a slower rate of ascent built into their models than the rate of ascent in the dive tables. The dive tables, for example, are based on a 60-foot-a-minute rate of ascent, while most computers use between 20- and 40-foot-a-minute rates of ascent. Exceeding the rate of ascent could cause you to get bent. The rate of ascent indicator is a warning device, often in the form of a blinking light or display that tells you if you are ascending faster than the built-in rate of ascent.

Ceiling Indicator

This feature is used when doing decompression dives. It indicates how far you can ascend without getting bent. The ceiling is the depth of your decompression stop. You can decompress at a depth deeper than the ceiling, as long as you are shallow enough to be outgassing.

Not all computers have ceiling indicators so obviously these cannot be used for decompression dives.

Decompression Mode Indicator

This feature indicates when you have exceeded the no-decompression time for your current depth and have entered a decompression mode. Decompression dives are beyond the realm of sport diving; once you enter into a decompression dive you can no longer ascend directly to the surface if you have an emergency.

Length of Decompression Time

Once again, this is an advanced feature that is not included on most computers designed for use by sport divers. This feature tells you how long you must decompress at your deepest or current level of outgassing before you can safely ascend to the surface.

Decompression time will shorten as you ascend to your ceiling since you are decompressing during your ascent.

✦ DIVING WITH A COMPUTER

The first consideration when diving with a computer is to keep in mind that the computer's program is based on a mathematical model, not your individual physiology. In practical terms this means do not dive the outer edges of your computer's program! If it tells you that you can go to 100 feet for twenty-five minutes, limiting your bottom time to twenty minutes would be prudent.

Obesity, fatigue, and being physically and/or mentally out of shape may all contribute to you being more susceptible to decompression sickness. Use the same common sense you were taught when using standard dive tables.

Ninety-five percent of all my diving is done with the computer. For this reason, I travel with two computers so anyone who dives with me is also using a computer. Sharing one computer could easily lead to disaster. It is not uncommon for one diver in a buddy team to drop 10 feet below his diving partner. Under no circumstances should you allow another diver to dive with you and follow your profile based on the computer you are using.

Obviously, the reverse is also true: you should not dive with someone who is using a computer and try to follow his profile instead of using the dive tables. If you do not have a computer, use the dive tables, regardless of what system your buddy is using.

Once you have done a dive with a computer, you cannot then do a future repetitive dive using standard dive tables. It is not possible to calculate accurately a repetitive dive later, based on any of the current computer readouts.

So what do you do if your computer blacks out or loses power after a dive? You stay out of the water for at least twelve hours, or forty-eight hours if you have been doing multiple deep dives or decompression dives.

If during a dive your computer shuts down, you should immediately ascend (at the recommended ascent rate) to 15 feet and use the remaining air (down to 500 psi, or less) for a safety stop. Do not attempt to "wing" the rest of the dive based on what you think the computer would be telling you.

Always do a safety stop at 15 feet for at least three minutes. New research suggests that this may be one of the most important things you can do to prevent decompression sickness. I now routinely use up a couple hundred psi doing a 15-foot safety stop at the end of all my dives regardless of depth, length, and whether or not it was the first dive of the day or the last of a series of repetitive dives.

Pay close attention to your rate of ascent. Computer models have the rate of ascent built into their parameters. If you ascend too fast, you risk bubble formation and decompression sickness. Standard dive tables are usually based on a 60-foot per minute rate of ascent. This is two to three times

Making a 15-foot safety stop is an excellent idea regardless of your dive profile.

Photo courtesy of Orca Industries.

faster than what many computers use. What you were taught about not ascending faster than the smallest exhaust bubble you can see will not work when diving with a computer.

Some dive computers can be used as decompression computers as opposed to no-decompression computers. Only professional divers should do decompression dives. Unless you are a professional diver, do not do decompression dives. The majority of computers on the market are designed as no-decompression computers. Sport divers should not make decompression dives.

Realize there is a difference between multilevel dive profiles and true decompression dives. Although a multilevel profile exceeds the bottom time standard dive tables would allow on the same dive, they are not true decompression dives because you can ascend directly to the surface at any time.

A multi-level dive profile refers to a dive that has two or more different dive depths during the same dive. These profiles acknowledge time spent at the shallower depth and credit the diver with more allowable bottom time. For example, a diver begins his dive at 100 feet, stays there for ten minutes, then ascends to 50 feet for ten minutes, and then ascends to 20 feet for twenty minutes. Standard dive tables would call this a 100-foot dive for forty minutes, which would be a decompression dive. The multilevel profile takes into account time spent at shallower depths, and time spent outgassing at the 20-foot mark, and so realizes this is not a decompression dive.

Once again, *do not do decompression dives*. You could define a decompression dive as any profile that would inhibit a direct ascent to the surface or exceeds the no-decompression time.

Avoid dives where you descend deep at the end of your dive. In other words, do not spend thirty minutes at 60 feet and then descend to 110 feet until you have used up your bottom time and then ascend to the surface. By taking advantage of outgassing in shallow water, where the last part of the dive should be spent, you can safely dive for longer periods of time. If you ascend directly from deep water, you have a higher risk of bubble formation and decompression sickness.

CHAPTER 16

Periodicals

The fact you're reading this book probably means you like to read about things that interest you! There are a number of excellent dive magazines on the market. These are some of the more popular.

⌁ *SKIN DIVER MAGAZINE*

Skin Diver comes out monthly and has a circulation of over 200,000; it is the biggest selling scuba publication around. Don't be fooled by the magazine's name; it is about scuba diving, not skin diving.

I recommend you subscribe to *Skin Diver*. The magazine has more information per issue than most of the other publications. Newly certified divers will benefit the most, especially if they're interested in obtaining information about where to go on a dive vacation.

Skin Diver carries more advertisements per issue than any other dive publication, and this is what critics of the magazine often complain about. Personally, I like all the advertisements—they're an excellent source of information about hotels and other types of dive travel particulars.

Skin Diver Magazine
6725 Sunset Blvd.
P.O. Box 3295
Los Angeles, CA 90099-2048

PACIFIC DIVER

Pacific Diver, as its name implies, covers scuba diving activities in the Pacific Ocean. The magazine is published bimonthly and is an excellent source of "local" information. I learn things from every issue of Pacific Diver.

One of the many aspects that make this magazine enjoyable is the fact that the people writing for it are truly "experts" and are currently active in the field. You won't find any "armchair" divers giving advice in the articles of Pacific Diver!

I particularly like the way Pacific Diver encourages pictures (in the "Pictorial" section) and stories (in the "Readers' Log Book" section) submitted by their readers; it is one of the features that contributes to the magazine being in tune with what local divers are up to.

Pacific Diver
P.O. Box 2027
Newport Beach, CA 92659-1027

SCUBA TIMES

Scuba Times magazine is published bimonthly and is a pleasant mix of dive travel, educational text on marine life, cold water diving, advanced diving, and more. In other words, a bit of everything in a very nice looking, clean package.

One of things I like about Scuba Times is the magazine's laid back feeling. It captures the feeling of relaxation most people experience when on a tropical vacation.

Scuba Times
P.O. Box 41094
Nashville, TN 37204-9905

OCEAN REALM

Some of the best underwater photography in the world can be seen in each issue of this beautiful (published quarterly) magazine. In fact, I often don't read the magazine until I've looked through it a couple of times because the photographs are so beautiful.

Ocean Realm doesn't have as much practical information as some of the other publications; it is definitely more of an "art" magazine. Ocean Realm is, however, probably the only dive magazine that can be equally enjoyed by non-divers.

If you want to turn someone on to the idea of becoming a diver, show them an issue of *Ocean Realm!*

Ocean Realm
342 West Sunset Road
San Antonio, TX 78209-1792

FISHEYE VIEW

Fisheye View is one of the smaller dive publications, but is growing fast.

What I like about *Fisheye View* is that it's well balanced: dive travel, product profiles, marine life, and environmental issues are all put together in a neat, easy to read format. Also, at $8.00 for a year's (six issues) subscription, *Fisheye View* is one of the best deals around!

Fisheye View
QL Tech Inc.
314 Romano Avenue
Coral Gables, FL 33134-7246

DIVE BOAT CALENDAR

Dive Boat Calendar is published bimonthly and lists schedules of dozens of dive boats. There are separate issues for the East and West coasts, so in subscribing you should specify what you want. Any diver who lives on one of these coasts should subscribe to this excellent source of information.

Dive Boat Calendar
17612 Beach Blvd.
Suite 20
Huntington Beach, CA 92647

DISCOVER DIVING

Discover Diving covers the diving scene on an international level, in conjunction with articles on underwater photography, marine life, interview/personality profiles, and general interest pieces.

The photography in the magazine is first rate and the articles are informative and well written; all in all, a terrific product.

Discover Diving
P.O. Box 83727
San Diego, CA 92138

➤ *TREASURE DIVER*

Treasure Diver started out as an "all treasure hunting" magazine, but has recently begun evolving into a more well-rounded publication.

At this writing, *Treasure Diver* doesn't feature any color photography at all (except for the cover). But if you're interested in treasure diving, shipwrecks, and related equipment, then this may be the magazine for you!

Treasure Diver
1111 Rancho Conejo Blvd.
Newbury Park, CA 91320

➤ *UNDERWATER USA*

Underwater USA is a bimonthly newspaper that supplies a lot of information.

It is easy to thumb through *Underwater USA* and get a quick feel for what the articles are about by the various headlines (just like you would with a regular newspaper). Like most newspapers, you'll find yourself selectively reading articles that catch your eye. One of the nice things about *Underwater USA* is that there is wide variety of topics in each issue.

Underwater USA
(800) 228-DIVE

➤ *SCUBAPRO DIVING & SNORKELING*

Scubapro Diving & Snorkeling is a mix of domestic and international scuba destination pieces, educational quizzes, and information about marine life.

Naturally, since the magazine is published by Scubapro, there's a lot of Scubapro advertising. This is not too bad since Scubapro makes great equipment.

Scubapro Diving & Snorkeling
P.O. Box 14003
Orange, CA 92613-9923

Glossary

ABSOLUTE PRESSURE—A combination of water and atmospheric pressure.

ALTERNATE AIR SUPPLY—A backup second stage, or a small backup tank.

AMBIENT LIGHT—Existing light, not strobe light.

AMBIENT PRESSURE—Surrounding water pressure.

ANOXIA—Lack of oxygen.

ARCHIMEDES' PRINCIPLE—Explains buoyancy—why things float and sink. States that an object's bouyancy is directly related to the weight of the water it displaces.

BACK SCATTER—Particles suspended in the water that are illuminated by the camera's flash.

BC—See *Buoyancy Compensator.*

BENDS—See *Decompression Sickness.*

BOOTIES—Neoprene (wetsuit) shoes, worn with fins that have a heel strap.

BOTTOM TIME—Length of time spent underwater during a dive.

BOW—The front of a boat.

BOYLE'S LAW—Explains the relationship between gas volume and pressure. States that assuming a constant temperature, pressure increases as volume decreases and pressure decreases as volume increases.

BUDDY—Companion during a dive.

BUDDY BREATHING—When two divers share one air supply. Usually refers to the act of passing a second stage back and forth.

BUOYANCY COMPENSATOR—A device that allows divers to adjust their buoyancy.

CAISSON'S DISEASE—See *Decompression Sickness.*

CERTIFICATION CARD—Proof that the holder has taken a scuba diving training course.

CLEARING YOUR MASK—Removing water from your mask while underwater.

COLOR ABSORPTION—Color from the light spectrum absorbed as it passes through water.

DALTON'S LAW—States that the total pressure exerted by a gas is equal to the sum of the individual gas pressures.

DECOMPRESSION SICKNESS—Formation of nitrogen or other inert gas in the blood vessels or body tissue as a result of supersaturation. Happens as a result of releasing pressure too quickly.

DEPTH GAUGE—A device that tells a diver how deep he is.

DIVE TABLES—Chart telling divers how long they can stay underwater without getting decompression sickness.

DRYSUIT—Environmental protection suit that keeps a person dry in the water.

EMBOLISM—A plug of air in the bloodstream, resulting from a break in the lungs when air in them overexpands. Usually caused by holding one's breath during an ascent.

EMERGENCY BUOYANT ASCENT—An ascent in which the diver is positively buoyant. Usually refers to an ascent made after the weight belt is dropped.

ENTANGLEMENTS—Anything that could entangle a diver underwater.

EQUALIZING—To take two unequal pressures and make them the same.

F.S.W.—Feet of Sea Water.

FREE SWIMMING ASCENT—Swimming to the surface. Usually refers to an emergency ascent made while wearing the weight belt.

GAME BAG—Bag to put things in, carried underwater by divers.

GAUGE CONSOLE—Houses the information gauges a diver uses.

HENRY'S LAW—States that a gas is soluble under pressure. Used to explain how nitrogen is absorbed and released in a diver's bloodstream and tissues.

HIGH PRESSURE PORT—Port for the submersible pressure gauge on the first stage of a regulator. Air from high pressure ports offers no reduction in tank pressure.

HYPERVENTILATION—The act of breathing fast and shallow.

IMMERSION SWITCH—On/off switch activated when wet.

INGASSING—The act of nitrogen being absorbed into a diver's body.

LIVE-ABOARDS—A dive boat that divers live on.

LIVE BOATING—Diving from a non-anchored boat.

LOW PRESSURE PORT—Pressure ports on the first stage of a regulator, which deliver air at a reduced pressure of about 140 psi.

MASK CLEARING—To remove the water from inside a mask underwater.

MASK SQUEEZE—When water pressure compresses the air space inside a mask.

MAXIMUM DEPTH INDICATOR—Shows the maximum depth attained during a dive.

MODELING LIGHT—Light used to compose a picture in low light situations.

MULTI-LEVEL DIVE PROFILE. A dive in which time is spent at more than one depth.

NARCED—See *Nitrogen Narcosis.*

NAUI—National Association of Underwater Instructors.

NITROGEN NARCOSIS—Condition brought about by breathing a high partial pressure of nitrogen. Makes divers feel inebriated, affects their judgment.

NO-DECOMPRESSION TIME—The amount of time a diver can spend underwater without having to decompress.

OUTGASSING—Nitrogen being released from the body.

PADI—Professional Association of Diving Instructors.

PORT—Left side of a boat.

POWER INFLATOR—Unit that pumps air from the scuba tank into the buoyancy compensator.

PSI—Pounds Per Square Inch.

PURGE VALVE—Device that allows you to purge water from a mask by blowing; usually on a mask or snorkel.

RAPTURE OF THE DEEP—See *Nitrogen Narcosis.*

RECOMPRESSION CHAMBER—Chamber used to reduce gas bubbles in the blood and body tissues by increasing air pressure.

REFRACTION—The bending of light as it passes from air to water.

SAFETY DIVER—Diver who is designated to perform rescues if needed.

SAFETY STOP—A stop made at a shallow depth to allow outgassing while still under pressure.

SCUBA—Self-Contained Underwater Breathing Apparatus.

SECOND STAGE—The part of a regulator that delivers air to the diver at ambient pressure. The part that goes in the diver's mouth.

SKIN DIVING—Swimming underwater without the use of scuba gear.

SKIP BREATHING—The dangerous practice of skipping every other breath while underwater to increase the amount of time a tank of air will last.

SPEAR GUN—Underwater gun powered by elastic bands or compressed air, used to hunt fish.

SSI—Scuba Schools International.

STARBOARD—Right side of a boat.

STERN—Back of a boat.

STROBE—Underwater camera flash.

SUBMERSIBLE PRESSURE GAUGE—Measures the amount of air in a scuba tank. Measures in pounds per square inch.

SWIM STEP—Step or ledge on the back of a boat used to assist people getting in and out of the water.

TTL—Through The Lens Metering.

VERTIGO—To be dizzy.

WEIGHT BELT—Weighted belt worn by divers to overcome the buoyancy of their gear and bodies.

WETSUIT—Environmental protection suit that insulates a diver by retaining a layer of water between the suit and the diver's body.

Index

A

Abalone, 103, 111–3
  Galley Ab Special, 112
  Seasick Special, 112
  Val's Abalone Cordon
    Bleu, 113
Absolute pressure, 43, 183
Absorption, color, 121, 184
Activities, non-diving, 139
Adjusted no-decompression
  time, 55
Adjusting equipment, 74–5
Age prerequisites, 21–2
Agents, travel, 152–4
Aids, underwater
  navigational, 76–7
Air, 47, 86–7, 173
  out of, 86–7
  will last, 173
Air, Spare, 86–7
Air embolism, 44–5, 92–4,
  184
AIR II, 100
Air supply, alternate, 86, 183
Air supply, secondary, 100
Alternate air supply, 86, 183
Altitude, 166–8
Aluminum tanks, 37
Ambient light, 183
Ambient pressure, 43, 183
A.N.D.T., see Adjusted
  no-decompression time
Anemones, strawberry,
  photo, 28
Angel shark, photo, 13
Anoxia, 183
Archimedes' Principle, 36, 37,
  46–7, 166, 183
Aruba, 140
ASA, 126
Ascents, 45, 87, 176, 184
  emergency, 45
  emergency buoyant, 87,
    184
  free swimming, 87, 184
  rate of, 176

Assassination, 15
Available light, 127–9

B

Back scatter, 131, 183
Bag, game, 40, 106, 184
  photo, 40
Bahamas, The, 150–2
Balanced regulator, 38
Barracuda, 18, 153, 161
  photo, 153
Basic course contents, 22
BC's, see Buoyancy
  compensators
Beach divers, 72
Beach diving, 109–10
Belt, weight, 36–7, 73, 186
Bends, 49–50, 53, 183
Bernard's Boiled Crab, 119
Bleeding, severe, 90–1
Block, reverse, 45
Bloodshot eyes, 46
Bloody Bay Wall, 145
Blue Holes, 139
Blue ringed octopus, 162
Blue sharks, photo, 109
Boat diving, 95–9
  entering the water, 99
Boating, live, 185
Boats, day, 96–9
Boats, dive, 16
Boiled Lobster, 113
Bonaire, 140–2
Booties, 31, 32–3, 183
  cost, 33
Bothidae, 103
Bottom time, 39, 55, 183
  total, 55
Bottom time/surface interval
  gauges, 39
Bottom timer, 172
Bow, 183
Boyle's Law, 37, 38, 44, 49, 50,
  183
Breaded Scallops, 120
Breathing, buddy, 86, 183

B.T., see Bottom time
Buck Island, 146–7
Buckles on masks, 31
Buddy, 71, 86, 88, 183
  breathing, 86, 183
  contact, lost, 88
  system, 71
Bug Diver, Darrel Allan'sTM,
  107
Bug hunting, see Lobster
  hunting
Buoyancy, 166
Buoyancy compensators,
  41–2, 47, 73, 77, 99, 183,
  184
  cost, 42
Buoyancy control, 77, 81–2
Buoyant ascents, emergency,
  87, 184
Butler Bay, 147

C

Calendar, Dive Boat, 97, 181
California bat ray, 11
California Grey Whale, 10
California hydro coral, photo,
  144
Camera, 122–3, 125
  housed movie, photo, 125
  housed system, 122–3
  Nikonos, 122
Camera controls, 133–4
Canon, 123
Capillary gauges, 38
Carbon dioxide, 47
Catalina Island, 11, 97, 142–3
Cave diving, 100
Cayman Islands, 79, 145–6,
  161
Ceiling indicator, 174
Certification, 19–24
  program, 19
  standards, 20–1
  time for, 22–3
Certification card, 22, 184
  junior, 22

Chamber, recompression, 185
Changes, pressure from
    depth, 76–7
Charisma, The, 93
Chem-lights, 107
Chipper's Crab Cake
    Surprise, 119
Classroom training, 22
Cleaning fish, 114–5
Clearing your mask, 30, 184,
    185
Clifton Wall, 151
Cod, 118
Collecting, game, *see* Game
    collecting
Colombia Reef, 149
Color absorption, 121, 184
Color loss, 52
Color separation, 127
Comfort level, 73–4
Compass, 39, 75–7
Compensators, buoyancy,
    41–2, 47, 184
Computer features, 171–4
Computer terminology,
    169–70
    M values, 170
    model, 169
    ongassing, 169–70
    outgassing, 169–70
    tissue half-times, 170
Computers, dive, *see* Dive
    computers
Congo Bay, 147
Console, gauge, 39–41, 75,
    184
Continued education, 77
Control, buoyancy, 77, 81–2
Controls, camera, 133–4
Cooking, 111–20
    abalone, 111–3
    crab, 119–20
    fish, 114–9
    lobster, 113–4
    scallops, 120
Coral, California hydro,
    photo, 144
Coral, fire, photo, 108
Coral gardens, photo, 148
Cordon Bleu, Val's Abalone,
    113
Coriolis, The, 95, 96
Cory's Sheephead Sunrise,
    117
Cost of equipment, 29, 31, 33,
    34, 35, 36, 37, 38, 42
Course, resort, 23
Course, contents, basic, 22
Cozumel, 149–50
CPR, 89, 90, 92
Crab Cake, Chipper's
    Surprise, 119

Crab, 119–20
    Bernard's Boiled, 119
    Chipper's Surprise, 119
    Lacroix's Cream Soup,
        119–20
Cramps, leg, 94
Curacao, 140
Customs, local, 137
Cuts, 90–1
Cyalume™ Chem-lights, 107

D
Dalton's Law, 47–9, 184
Dams, 165
DAN, *see* Divers Alert
    Network
Darrel Allan's Bug Diver™,
    107
Day boats, 96–9
Decompression dives, 177
Decompression mode
    indicator, 174
Decompression sickness,
    49–50, 53, 91–2, 184
Deep, rapture of the, 51, 185
Depth changes, pressure
    from, 76–7
Depth gauges, 38–9, 167, 172,
    184
    oil-filled, 38
Depth indicator, maximum,
    38–9, 185
Discover Diving, 181–2
Dives, 9–18, 54, 56–69
    first, 56–60
    non-repetitive, 54
    repetitive, 54
    second, 60–9
    why, 9–18
Dive Boat Calendar, 97, 181
Dive boats, 16
Dive computers, 41, 75, 168,
    169–77
    diving with a, 175–7
    features, 171–4
    sharing, 175
    terminology, 169–70
Dive profile, multi-level, 185
Dive specialties, 95–110
    beach diving, 109–10
    boat diving, 95–9
    cave diving, 100
    day boats, 96–9
    game collecting, 102–6
    ice diving, 100–2
    night diving, 106–11
    wreck diving, 99–100
Dive stores, 25–8
    incentives in, 26
    instructors at, 26–7
    location of, 25–6
    personnel at, 27–8

Dive stores, *continued*
    rental department of, 26
    service at, 27
    type of, 27
Dive tables, 53–69, 167–8,
    184
    NAUI, chart, 54
    terminology of, 53–5
    using, 55–69
Dive travel, 135–54
    travel agents, 152–4
    where to go, 139–54
Diver, safety, 186
Diver, self-sufficient, 71–9
Diver, thinking, 78–9
Diver, unconscious, 89–90
Diver's Alert Network, 137–8
Divers, safety, 101–2
Dives, decompression, 177
Diving, 9–18, 44, 50–1, 70, 72,
    95–102, 106–10, 163–8,
    186
    beach, 72, 109–10
    boat, 95–9
    cave, 100
    flying after, 50–1
    fresh water, 163–8
    ice, 100–2
    night, 106–9
    pollution, 14–5
    skin, 44, 106, 186
    surf, photo, 70
    why, 9–18
    wreck, 97, 99–100
        photo, 97
Diving above sea level, 50
Diving with a computer,
    175–7
Dizziness, 84–6
Drowning, 90
Dry suits, 35–6, 101, 184
    cost, 36

E
Eagle Ray Alley, 145
Eardrum, ruptured, 46, 86
Eastern Airlines, 139
Ebo's Reef, 141
Education, continued, 77
Eels, moray, 82, 158, 159
    photo, 158
Ektachrome, 126
Electric ray, 157, 161
    torpedo ray, photo, 157
Embolisms, 44–5, 92–4, 184
Emergencies, 71, 84–90
    entanglements, 87–8
    lost buddy contact, 88
    out of air, 71, 84–6
    surface rescues, 88–9
    unconscious diver, 89–90
    vertigo, 84–6

Emergency ascents, 45, 87, 184
  buoyant, 87, 184
Entanglements, 85, 87–8, 184
  photo, 85
Entering the water, boat diving, 99
Environment, causing stress, 82
Environments, fresh water, 164–6
Equalizing, 45, 184
Equipment, 29–42, 74–5, 81–2, 122–3
  adjusting, 74–5
  causing stress, 81–2
  dive computers, 41
  drysuits, 35–6
  fins, 31–2
  gauges, 38–41
  gloves, 34
  knives, 42
  masks, 29–31
  photography, 122–3
  regulators, 38
  snorkels, 33–4
  tanks, 37
  weight belts, 36–7
  wetsuits, 34–5
Eustachian tube, 45
Evacuation, helicopter, 93, 94
  photo, 93
Eyes, bloodshot, 46

F
Fears of marine life, 155
Fiji, 95
Fijikawa Maru, 145
Fillets, 116–8
Film, 123–7
  ASA, 126
  Kodachrome™ 64, 124
Filming, photo, 16
Films, 15
Fins, 31–2
  cost, 31
  full foot, 31
  small body surfing, 31, 32
  with heel straps, 32
Fire coral, photo, 108
First aid, 81–94
  cuts and severe bleeding, 90–1
  decompression sickness, 91–2
  drowning, 90
  embolisms, 92–4
  hyperthermia, 92
  hypothermia, 92
  leg cramps, 94
  seasickness, 94
  shock, 91

First dive, 56–60
Fish, 103–6, 114–9
  cleaning, 114–5
  flat, 103–6
  Halibut, 118–9
  Rockfish, 115–6
Fish fillets, 116–8
  Cory's Sheephead Sunrise, 117
  Fried Garlic, 117
  Greenfield Special, 116
  Grilled, 117
  Grilled with Nuts and Cheese, 117
  Trauer's Cod and Tomatoes Special, 118
Fish stringer, 106
Fisherman, spear, 106
Fisheye View, 181
Flash lights, 42
Flash photography, 129–31
Flat fish, 103–6
Flying after diving, 50–1
Focusing, 133
Free swimming ascent, 87, 184
French Cap Cay, 147
Fresh water diving, 163–8
  altitude, 166–8
  buoyancy, 166
  environments, 164–6
Fresh water environments, 164–6
Fried Garlic Fish, 117
Full foot fins, 31

G
Galley Ab Special, 112
Game bags, 40, 106, 184
  photo, 40
Game collecting, 102–6
  abalone, 103
  flat fish, 103–6
  lobster, 102–3
  scallops, 103
Gauge consoles, 39–41, 75, 184
Gauges, 38–41, 75, 167, 172, 184, 186
  bottom time/surface interval, 39
  capillary, 38
  depth, 38–9
  oil-filled depth, 38
  submersible pressure, 39, 186
Gear, dive, photo, 36
Gear, modern scuba, 14
Gear, personal, 29
Giant striated, 72
Ginni Springs, 163
Glossary, 183–6

Gloves, 30, 34
  cost, 34
Greenfield Special, The, 116
Grilled Fish Fillets, 117
Grilled Fish Fillets with Nuts and Cheese, 117
Grilled Lobster, 114
Grilled Scallops, 120
Group letter, 55

H
Half-times, tissue, 170
Halibut, 118–9
  Heidi's Special, 118
  Pierre's Grilled with Pasta, 118–9
Hang-off tank, photo, 76
Heat underwater, 52
Heidi's Halibut Special, 118
Helicopter evacuation, 93, 94
  photo, 93
Hellcat, photo, 12
Henry's Law, 49, 50, 184
High volume masks, 30
Hotel location, 135
Housed system, 28, 122–3, 125
  camera, photo, 28
  movie camera, photo, 125
Hunting, lobster, 102–3
Hunting, underwater, 101, 102–6
  photo, 101
"Hydro," 37
Hyperthermia, 92
Hyperventilation, 83, 185
Hypothermia, 92

I
Ice diving, 100–2
Ikelite, 75
Immersion switch, 171, 185
Indicator, maximum depth, 38–9, 185
Instructors, at dive stores, 26–7
Instructors, dive, photo, 24
Insurance, 137
International Pier, 150
Interval, surface, 55, 69
  planning, 69

J
Jackson Point, 145
Jaws 3, 152
Jelly Fish Lake, photo, 41
Junior certification card, 22

K
Keepers, weight belt, 37
Kelp, 82
Knife, dive, photo, 41

Knives, 42
Kodachrome™ 64, 124, 126, 131

L
Lacroix's Cream of Crab Soup, 119–20
Lakes, 164
Leg cramps, 94
Length of decompression time, 174
Level, comfort, 73–4
Light, modeling, 185
Light underwater, 52, 127–9, 183
    ambient, 183
    available, 127–9
Lines, safety, 100
Lionfish, 157, 158
    photo, 158
Live-aboards, 95, 96, 98, 135–6, 185
Lobster, 101, 113–4
    Boiled, 113
    Grilled, 114
    photo, 101
    Soup, Michel's, 114
Lobster hunting, 102–3
Local customs, 137
Long Point, 142
Lorraine's Underwater Special, 120
Lost buddy contact, 88
Low battery power indicator, 173–4
Low volume masks, 30

M
M values, 170
Mail, shopping by, 28
Mako shark, photo, 153
Manual strobe, 130
Manual switch, 171
Maracaibo Reef, 150
Marine Life, 82, 155–62, 163
    barracuda, 161
    causing stress, 82
    electric ray, 161
    fears of, 155
    moray eels, 159
    octopus, 162
    scorpionfish, 157–9
    sea snakes, 162
    sharks, 156–7
    stonefish, 159
    whales, 162
Mask squeeze, 46, 185
Masks, 29–31, 72–3, 81, 184
    buckles on, 31
    clearing your, 30, 184
    cost, 31
    high volume, 30
    low volume, 30

Maximum depth indicator, 38–9, 185
Medical considerations, 137–8
Michel's Lobster Soup, 114
Minolta, 123
Model, 169
Mola Mola, photo, 156
Monk's Haven, 141
Moray eels, 82, 158, 159
    photo, 158
Mouth-to-mouth resuscitation, 89
Muscle tension, 83

N
Narcosis, Nitrogen, 51, 185
Narrowing, psychological, 83
Nassau, 150
National Association of Underwater Instructors (NAUI), 19, 21, 50, 53, 54, 55, 167, 168, 185
    dive tables, chart, 54
Navigational aids, underwater, 76–7
N.D.T., see No-decompression time
Never Say Never, 151
New Providence Island, 150–1
New Tarpon Alley, 145
Ngemelis, 140
Night diving, 106–10
Night photography, 131–3
    focusing, 133
    strobes, 132
Nikon F3, photo, 125
Nikonos, 133
Nikonos system, 122
Nikonos V, 122, 124
    photo, 124
Nippo Maru, 142–3
Nitrogen, 47, 49, 53, 55, 169
    absorption, 169
    release, 169
    time, residual, 53, 55
Nitrogen narcosis, 51, 185
No-decompression time, 50, 54–5, 172–3, 185
    adjusted, 55
    for repetitive dives, 172–3
Non-diving activities, 139
Non-penetration wreck diving, 99–100
Non-repetitive dive, 54

O
Ocean Realm, 180–1
Octopus, 9, 160, 162
    photo, 160
Oil-filled depth gauges, 38
Ongassing, 169–70

On/off switches, 171
Open water training, 22
Out of air, 71, 86–7
    emergency, 71
Outgassing, 169–70
Oxygen, 47

P
Pacific Diver, 180
Pad, spine, 35
PADI, see Professional Association of Diving Instructors
Palancar Reef, 150
Palau, 11, 18, 36, 100, 139–40, 168
    photo, 168
Paradise Island, 151
Passports, 136
Pasta, Scallop, 120
Pentax, 123
Periodicals, 179–82
Personal gear, 29
    cost, 29
Personnel at dive stores, 27–8
Photographing shipwreck, photo, 17
Photography, 121–34
    available light, 127–9
    color absorption, 121
    equipment, 122–3
    film, 123–7
    flash, 129–31
    night, 131–3
    other camera controls, 133–4
    plan your shot, 134
Pierre's Grilled Halibut with Pasta, 118–9
Planning your surface interval, 69
Pollution, 14–5
Ponds, 165–6
Pool training, 22
Power inflator, 185
Power source, 171–2
Prerequisites for training, 21–2
    age, 21–2
President Coolidge, 17, 18, 141
    photos, 17, 141
Pressure, 43, 183
    absolute, 43, 183
    ambient, 43, 183
Pressure from depth changes, 76–7
Pressure gauges, submersible, 39, 186
Pressure port, high, 185
Pressure port, low, 185
Professional Association of Diving Instructors, 20, 21, 53, 185

Program, certification, 19
PSI, 185
Psychological narrowing, 83
Purge valve, 30, 34, 185

Q
Quarries, 165

R
Rapture of the deep, 51, 185
Rate of ascent, 174, 176
    indicator, 174
Ray, California bat, 11
Ray, electric, 157, 161
    photo, 157
Recompression chamber, 185
Refraction, 186
Regulators, 38, 72
    balanced, 38
    cost, 38
Rental department of dive
    stores, 26
Repetitive dive, 54
Reppel, 141
Rescue work, 15
Rescues, surface, 88–9
Residual nitrogen time, 53, 55
Resorts, 15, 23
Resuscitation, mouth to
    mouth, 89
Reverse block, 45
Ripples in sand, 76
Rivers, 164
R.N.T., see Residual nitrogen
    time
Rockfish, 115–6
    Rocky's, 116
    Salad, 116
    Steamed, 115
Rocky's Rockfish, 116
Ruptured eardrum, 46, 86

S
Safety divers, 101, 186
Safety lines, 100
Safety stop, 175–6, 186
    photo, 176
St. Croix, 146–9
St. John, 146–9
St. Lawrence River, 14
St. Thomas, 146–9
Salad, Rockfish, 116
Salt Flats, 141
Sand, ripples in, 76
Sand "Chute," 151
Santa Monica Bay, 14
Scallops, 103, 105, 120
    Breaded, 120
    Grilled, 120
    Lorraine's Underwater
        Special, 120
    Pasta, 120
    photo, 105

Scatter, back, 131, 183
Scorpionfish, 157–9
Scuba, 186
Scuba gear, modern, 14
Scuba Schools International,
    20, 53, 186
Scuba Times, 180
Scubapro Diving & Snorkeling,
    182
Sea level, diving above, 50
Sea lions, 18, 128
    photo, 128
Sea snakes, 162
Seasick Special, 112
Seasickness, 94
Second dive, 60–9
Second stage, 186
Secondary air supply, 100
Self-sufficient diver, 71–9
Separation, color, 127
Service at dive stores, 27
Shark suits, steel mesh, photo,
    32
Sharks, 10, 13, 109, 153, 156–7
    angel, photo, 13
    blue, photo, 109
    mako, photo, 153
Sheephead, 117
Shinkoku Maru, 143
Ship Rock, 142
Shipwreck, photos, 17, 79
Shock, 91
Shopping by mail, 28
S.I., see Surface interval
Sickness, decompression,
    49–50, 53, 91–2, 184
Silhouettes, 127–9, 132
    photo, 132
Six-packs, 16, 99
Skin Diver Magazine, 179
Skin diving, 44, 106, 186
Slave strobes, 133–4
Smith, J.L.B., 159
Snakes, sea, 162
Snorkel, 33–4, 72
    cost, 34
Soles on booties, 32
Sound underwater, 51–2
Soup, Lacroix's Cream of
    Crab, 119–20
Soup, Michel's Lobster, 114
Spare Air, 86–7
Spear fishermen, 106
Specialties, dive, see Dive
    specialties
SPG, see Submersible
    pressure gauges
Spine pad, 35
Springs, 164
Squeeze, mask, 46, 185
SSI, see Scuba Schools
    International
Standards, certification, 20–1

Steamed Rockfish, 115
Steel mesh shark suit,
    photo, 32
Steel tanks, 37
Step, swim, 186
Stingray City, 145
Stingrays, 157
Stonefish, 159
Stop, safety, 175–6, 186
    photo, 176
Stores, dive, see Dive stores
Strawberry anemones, photo,
    28
Streams, 166
Stress, diver's, 81–4
    caused by environment, 82
    caused by equipment,
        81–2
    dealing with, 83–4
    symptoms of, 83
Striated, giant, 72
Stringer, fish, 106
Strobes, 121, 130, 132, 133–4,
    186
    manual, 130
    slave, 133–4
    underwater, 121
Submersible pressure gauges,
    39, 75, 186
Sue–jack, 142
Sunfish, photo, 156
Supplies, alternate air, 86, 183
Supply, secondary air, 100
Surf diving, photo, 70
Surf line, 110
Surface interval time, 55, 69,
    172
    planning, 69
Surface rescues, 88–9
Swim step, 186
Swimming ascent, free, 87,
    184
Switch, immersion, 185
Switches, on/off, 171

T
Tables, dive, see Dive tables
Tank, hang-off, photo, 76
Tank pressure, 173
Tanks, 37
    cost, 37
T.B.T., see Total bottom time
Tears of Allah, 151
Temperature, 173
Tension, muscle, 83
Terminology, computer,
    169–70
Terminology, dive tables,
    53–5
Theory, 43–52
    air, 47
    Archimedes' Principle,
        46–7

Theory, *continued*
  Boyle's Law, 44
  Dalton's Law, 47–9
  heat underwater, 52
  Henry's Law, 49
  light underwater, 52
  pressure, 43
  sound underwater, 51–2
Thinking diver, 78–9
Thunderball, 152
Time, 39, 50, 53, 54–5, 172, 183, 185
  adjusted no-compression, 55
  bottom, 39, 55, 183
  no decompression, 50, 54–5, 185
  residual nitrogen, 53, 55
  surface interval, 172
  total bottom, 55
Timer, bottom, 172
Tissue half-times, 170
Total bottom time, 55
Training, 21–2
  classroom, 22
  open water, 22
  pool, 22
  prerequisites for, 21–2
Transportation, 126–7
Trauer's Cod and Tomatoes Special, 118
Travel, dive, 11–2, 135–54
  free, 12
Travel agents, 152–4
Treasure Diver, 182
Trinity Caves, 151
Truk Lagoon, 11, 143–5

Turtle Farm, 146

U
U.S. Navy Dive Tables, 50, 53, 79, 167
Unconscious diver, 89–90
Underwater hunting, 101, 102–6
  photo, 101
Underwater navigational aids, 76–7
Underwater Park, 142
Underwater strobe, 121
Underwater USA, 182

V
Vacations, 135–9
  hotel location, 135
  insurance, 137
  local customs, 137
  medical considerations, 137–8
  non-diving activities, 139
  passports and visas, 136
  transportation, 136–7
  vaccinations, 137
  what you need, 138
  where to stay, 135–6
Vaccinations, 137
Val's Abalone Cordon Bleu, 113
Valves, purge, 30, 34, 185
Vanuatu, 95
Vasoconstriction, 92
Vertigo, 45–6, 84–6, 186
Virgin Islands, 146–9
Visas, 136

W
Wakulla Springs, 164
Waterfalls, 166
Weight belt keepers, 37
Weight belts, 36–7, 73, 186
  cost, 37
Weights, 36, 74–5
  cost, 36
Wetsuits, 34–5, 81, 186
  cost, 35
  problems with, 81
Whales, 10, 14, 162
  California Grey, 10
Where to go, 139–54
  Bahamas, 150–2
  Bonaire, 140–2
  Catalina Island, 142–3
  Cayman Islands, 145–6
  Cozumel, 149–50
  Palau, 139–40
  Truk Lagoon, 143–5
  Virgin Islands, 146–9
Why dive, 9–18
Wide Angle Non TTL, 130
Wide Angle TTL, 129–30
Wonder Channel, 140
Wreck diving, 97, 99–100
  photo, 97

Z
Zebrafish, 157
Zippers on booties, 32–3
Zippers on gloves, 34
Zodiacs, 96, 99